CLEAN OUT YOUR LIFE CLOSET

Copyright © 2016 by Corbie Mitleid

ALL RIGHTS RESERVED.
This book or any portion thereof may not be reproduced or used in any manner whatsoever without the express written permission of the publisher except for the use of brief quotations in a book review.

Contact information at https://corbiemitleid.com/contact

Cover Design: Alexander von Ness
Editor: Berni Xiong

978-1-61468-370-4

*For Amy —
Thanks for doing
the rough stuff!*

CLEAN OUT YOUR LIFECLOSET

THE SELF-DEVELOPMENT PROJECT

— Corbie Mitleid

CORBIE MITLEID

Dedication

*Dedicated to my father,
Jerome R. Dorkin, MD (1921-2001):*

Best friend, cheering section, slayer of NY Times Crossword Puzzles (in ink), brilliant and compassionate physician, punster extraordinaire. The man who taught me to remain eternally unfinished, always looking for new answers and asking the next question. If I'm any kind of writer, it's because of your love affair with words well-crafted. I miss having you "in form" with us, but cherish the fact that you're still around me in spirit. I love you.

Contents

Foreword — 1

Reviews — 5

Preface:
I'll Show You Mine If You Show Me Yours — 11

Introduction:
How To Be a Martian
Without Leaving Earth — 15

About The Self-Development Project — 17

Part I:
Getting Clear

The Joy of a Clear Telescope — 23

Getting Clear On Your Purpose — 33

Getting Clear In Your Relationships — 43

Getting Clear With Spirit — 57

Part II:
Simplicity and Living Well With Less

Life As a Tiny House — 69

Finding Happiness With
What You Have Right Now — 83

Carry Experiences, Not Things — 95

What To Do With Stuff
When You've Lightened Your Load — 105

Part III: Going With the Flow, Learning To Adapt

Why Perfect Isn't What You Think It Is — 117

Stumbling Toward Enlightenment — 125

How Perfect Destroys Good — 135

When To Stand Your Ground — 145

Part IV: Stress Is a Complicated Friend

Is Stress Good Or Bad? — 157

Stress As the Shot Across the Bow — 167

Stress As Mission Creep — 177

Stress, the Donkey, and
the Hole In the Ground — 187

Conclusion — 197

Wingfolks — 201

Aknowledgements — 205

About the Author — 207

Foreword

By David Bennett

In my experience of coaching others, I have had the opportunity to speak to people from all around the world. I've found that we all are searching for a sense of peace and understanding. In these challenging times, we find ourselves looking everywhere but in the most important place—within ourselves. When working on developing into a better person, we sometimes come to a limit of our understanding. When we reach these boundaries, we find ourselves in an emotional realm that leads us to confusion. Now we can either step back or push forward. I prefer to move forward locating the tools needed to find solid footing and emerge from the fog with new understanding, allowing this focused zone to percolate into a new authentic self. After reading *Clean Out Your LifeCloset,* I can clearly see this book provides the tools needed to create that focus and direction in your life.

I've known Corbie Mitleid for many years and enjoy our discussions about the empowering and practical ways we can live our lives. She views life with a fresh outlook—believing life's circumstances are open to all possible explanations—and she has successfully brought that inspiring view to this work. She shows the reader how to find enthusiasm for life, to look forward to change, and to grow while experiencing it. She teaches you to allow yourself to be of service with heart-centered authenticity because you are excited about the promise life holds. You'll discover how to give up anxiety and fear, yet hold an intention of a brighter tomorrow that fills you with overflowing gratitude and love.

We are all living a personal story—each with its ups and downs, and high and low points. But what's important is the theme that structures and guides your story. When your story has positive, life-supporting themes, you have found the key to transformation. From time to time we may need to add new vigor to our disciplines, so they maintain a fresh vitality. Each chapter offers ways to reframe your world and make it sparkle. We live in a paradigm of heroic individuals struggling over limited resources, yet do we always need the biggest, the fastest, or the best? We need a new story to live in harmony and within our means. Science is showing us that we are connected to each other in many ways. We would be better served by establishing cooperation and building dynamic relationships.

Within this first book of three, we learn to cultivate an attitude of simplicity in our own life by eliminating unnecessary activities and preoccupations. Simplifying life allows us to develop a genuine mental discipline toward loving kindness with less distraction. Like an upper branch growing out of a tree, strive to live simply because the tip of the branch cannot hold the weight of too much *stuff*.

As we simplify our lives, we have more time and energy to help others and realize our lightened life on the top.

Read on to find the help you need to rise above the circumstances and remove yourself from the same old rut. No matter how beautiful the rut may be, you cannot see above the furrow to the expansive possibilities that await you. Remember that every moment of possibility resides in *this* moment, and you have the capacity to clean house so your future can become a shining beacon.

DAVID BENNETT
Author of Voyage of Purpose and
A Voice as Old as Time (DharmaTalks.com)

Reviews

"Corbie is the Marie Kondo of the heart and soul, helping us to honor those long-held emotional hang-ups that no longer serve us, then let them go, cleansing our spirits for new experiences and greater joys. A wonderful book to reread again and again."

- SHANNON HAYES
*Author of Radical Homemakers:
Reclaiming Domesticity from a Consumer Culture,
and Long Way on a Little: An Earth Lover's Companion
for Enjoying Meat, Pinching Pennies and Living Deliciously*

"If you find yourself stumbling, tripping or falling towards enlightenment, *Clean Out Your LifeCloset* is an outstanding primer to give you more clarity and insight in your life. Corbie Mitleid has written a treasure trove woven full of golden stories, powerful tools and useful techniques—and a little practical magic too. *Clean Out Your LifeCloset* is the book that you didn't even know that you've been looking for to integrate a new breed of self-development into your life, especially if you're a mere mortal like the rest of us!"

- BLAZE LAZARONY
CEO & Founder, Blaze A Brilliant Path

"Volumes have been written on the topic of attaining and living a fuller, more complete life. *Clean Out Your LifeCloset* pares away the rhetoric and resonates with 'complex simplicity' that truly defines the process. Regardless of whether you define your self as expert or novice, the words and ideas in this plainly written, well-told story will enrich your Authentic Life."

- PAMELA STEELE
*Artist/Mage/Author of Steele Wizard Tarot
and Wizard's Pets Tarot*

"Often used in this book is the word 'clear' and indeed that's where the readers are taken: on a journey to clearly define what they want and need for their lives and a clear path to attaining it. Written in an easy to follow yet inspirational manner, *Clean Out Your LifeCloset* is a volume readers will keep and return to when life gets cloudy."

- DONNA CORNELL
Philanthropist and CEO, Cornell Enterprises

"Witty, insightful, and fun. In *Clean Out Your LifeCloset*, Corbie Mitleid gently cajoles her readers to explore life through a new and refreshing lens: that of the soul and the spiritual heart. A great read for anyone who wants to live a more meaningful and inspired life."

- MARTHA G. BLESSING, RN
Author of God Is A Pink Cloud: Crossing the Spiritual Bridge from Chronic Pain and Illness to Health, Happiness and Inner Peace; Founder of Soul Light Healing Academy

"With crystal clarity and wit, Corbie Mitleid offers a wealth of practical, down-to-earth wisdom to help you create the life of your dreams. Highly recommended."

- ROBERT SCHWARTZ
*Between Lives Soul Regression Therapist;
Author of Your Soul's Plan: Discovering the Real Meaning of the Life You Planned Before You Were Born, and Your Soul's Gift: The Healing Power of the Life You Planned Before You Were Born*

"Corbie Mitleid has written a gem of a book. While you may 'read' it in one day, it will take years to master the many juicy and empowering tidbits that are outlined throughout the volume. It is high time we all cleaned out and arranged our personal closet to suit our lifestyle and desires. Come ready to change, and get ready to dog-ear a bounty of pages with your highlighter!"

- CHRISTINE ALEXANDRIA
Author of Askfirmations: Live the Life You Desire Simply by Asking, The Angel Chatter Oracle Cards, and the award-winning, Pick-A-Woowoo: Have You Ever Wondered About Angels?

"*Clean Out Your LifeCloset* is a fun, creative, imagination-filled, practical self-help book that is an easy read, down to earth, with no 'fuzzy bunnies' or wishy washy unattainable goals. I loved the experiments and exercises offered to the reader. What a great practical way to embody the book's message!"

- ANIIYAH KLOCK
Licensed Massage Therapist and Energy Healer

"For years, Corbie Mitleid has stood out as an enlightened and gifted teacher and writer. Written in her trademark entertaining style, *Clean Out Your LifeCloset* skillfully delivers soul wisdom and encourages us to let go of that which impedes our spiritual advancement and path to internal joy and peace. If you desire to live your life in clarity and balance, this first volume of humorous Sage wisdom is a powerful tool and highly recommended for your journey. *Clean Out Your LifeCloset* is the kind of unique and delightful read you will want for those you care about most, beginning with you."

- TED SILVERHAND
Tuscarora Native Seer

"With *Clean Out Your LifeCloset*, Corbie Mitleid gives you a guide for self-examination and introspection from the heart's vantage point. This book gives you the tools and techniques that are designed especially for each person who reads it. This will become your resource book for Life."

- CAROLINE CHANG
Producer & Host, Awake 2 Oneness Radio and Founder & Director, The KYLE Foundation, Inc.

"Before you set on paving your own path in life, you need to find out who you truly are, what makes you unique, and what you have to contribute to the world. *Clean Out Your LifeCloset* is a great combination of insight, illustrative stories, and practical advice to give you the best opportunity to reveal your true essence. Corbie Mitleid's wisdom and wit shine through and make this book a must-read for anyone on a road of self-discovery."

- DIANA TUMMINIA, LCSW-R
Mental Health Practitioner and Psychotherapist

"Such a wonderful marriage of wisdom and wit. So thoughtful, well-written and easy to read, *Clean Out Your LifeCloset* is filled with helpful metaphors, examples and stories to bring the principles brilliantly to life—and worksheets to help you dive even deeper. If you're ready to not only think, but also fully LIVE outside the box, this book will be a treasured guide!"

- RUTH L. SCHWARTZ
Author of Soul on Earth: A Guide to Living and Loving Your Human Life

"*Clean Out Your LifeCloset* offers practical, doable, sensible techniques that create ideal conditions for personal transformation and growth. Corbie writes in pictures. Her voice is colorful and dynamic, her words a joy to read."

- VANESSA GOBES
Cofounder, Chrysalis Meditation Center (InsideTheChrysalis.com)

"In our modern world, we as individuals are submersed in a sense of self-induced complicatedness. In *Clean Out Your LifeCloset*, Corbie Mitleid shows us how the simplification of our lives in all aspects leads to clarity, which in turn leads to an enlightened life. It is essentially a road map out of our self-induced complicatedness where the road and the map are the individual at the same time."

- LORRIE STOJNI
Mother, Family Law Lawyer, and Healer

"*Clean Out Your LifeCloset* brings the reader a different slant on clearing out Life's clutter. Deeply useful in accepting responsibility for one's own life experiences and the need to find one's own presence in a world that suffers from non-consciousness and focuses on material needs and wants. A wonderful reminder that we are merely spiritual beings having a human adventure."

- MICHELE KELEHER, MS, PT
Energy Medicine Practitioner

"Most of us move through life looking through a clouded window, seeing what's right in front of us but never the whole picture. When it comes to our feelings, thoughts, and responses, we don't ask ourselves 'why?' Instead, we act on impulse and move on. *Clean Out Your LifeCloset* isn't about changing who you are, but about getting to know yourself and growing into the best version of you. Optimal human functioning, self-actualization, happiness, whatever you like to call it, can be achieved if you're willing to do the work. And while author Corbie Mitleid doesn't claim to have all the answers, her book can help you find them."

- HEATHER BESCHIZZA
Adjunct Professor of Psychology, Community College of Allegheny County; ESL Instructor, Duquesne University

Preface:
I'll Show You Mine If You Show Me Yours

Tell me if you've heard *this* one before: A guy intent on Change walks into a coffee bar, which happens to be attached to a bookstore. The guy forgets all about the coffee as row upon row of "I've-Got-Your-Answer" tomes call to him, siren-like, from the soaring bookshelves.

If you're like me, you're someone who believes that there's always room to change, to grow, and to learn. And all that changing, growing, and learning is fun—or ought to be. But if you take a good look at your own bookshelves, I bet you've got somewhere between dozens and hundreds of New Age and self-help volumes that you haven't even read.

These books look terrific in the store. They have sexy titles, good cover art, and delicious-sounding tables of contents. The back-cover recommendation blurbs sing the author's praises. And as you flip through this one or that one, a paragraph or exercise catches your eye. You think, *Hmmm...maybe this is the one that will work!* So you buy it and bring it home. Perhaps it sits on your "to read" shelf or your bedside table for a while. You skim a chapter or two when you have a little time, but for some reason, the book just doesn't grab you the way it did in the store. And so it goes into your general library—to silently remind you that you "Still Haven't Found What You're Looking For," (thank you, U2).

Guess what? Me, too. And I've been buying these promising volumes and bringing them home for almost forty years. From the books in the 1970s that promised to make me a thin, sexy, and datable teenager, to recent ones that promised to make me thin, sexy and happily married post-menopause—not to mention compassionate, worldly-wise, activist, mindful, abundant, fearless, and happy in 350 pages or less. And except for a beloved and dog-eared handful, they remain unread.

However, what all those volumes—read and unread—*have* done is prove that the only one who has answers for me is me.

"So, smart gal," you're saying, "if that's true, why should I buy *your* book?"

Simple. It's not just mine—it's yours. Without your participation, this book is only half-written.

I've experienced successes and failures. I've been fast tracked and shoved into the parking lot. I've had days where I *got* to get up in the morning and days when I *had* to (quite a difference, let me tell you). And along the way I learned, figured out what did and didn't work for me, and realized that all the self-help books in the world don't do a thing if they don't speak to who you are in every detail of your life.

The Self-Development Project series is my chance to share my own journey with you, without preaching "this is what you *have to* do." (You'll notice that the word *must* is rarely used in this book.) Instead, I want to inspire you to take your own journey, without comparing it to mine as an author or anyone else's around you. Because everyone's experiences or challenges are different, it follows that any healing journey taken by my readers will also be unique. One of the ways to find healing is through self-knowledge: understanding *why* you do what you do and *how* that brings certain events into your life. But what those answers *are* will totally and completely be up to *You*.

So, you're writing this book with me, every step of the way. In the essays and exercises that follow, you'll learn how to play: with yourself, with ideas, with the whole notion of "only one way to get it right." And at the end of the journey, you'll be able to truly own the fact that you have your own answers—you've had them all along!

Ready? Let's romp!

Introduction: How To Be a Martian Without Leaving Earth

My father, Jerome Dorkin, was a physician back in the 1950s and 1960s when doctor visits were still two dollars, evening office hours were normal, and house calls were commonplace. His small one-man office was attached to the house via a door in our kitchen. I loved wandering in when Dad wasn't busy because the big examining table had a huge roll of paper on it. Technically, it was for the patients: each one got a fresh covering for the table before they'd climb on. But for me, that big roll of paper was magic waiting to happen.

On rare occasions, my father would tear off a six-foot length and tape it to my wall. I would then proceed to go to town, drawing figures and scribbling stories to my heart's content. No coloring books for me—too small! And why color in the lines anyway? I had bigger visions than that. Those days with unlimited paper and boundless imagination are some of my best childhood memories.

That's why I love thinking like a Martian.

No, that doesn't mean running around with a scrubbing brush on my Roman-style helmet and big sneakers. I leave that version to Looney Tunes.

Rather, it involves observing the world as if I am an explorer from another planet. It's an unlimited state of mind that encourages me to leave my judgments at the door of any experience.

Here's an example: I am sitting across from a man who has tears running down his face. There is no verifiable stimulus for this action. There are two questions I can ask to address this:

"Why are you crying?" assumes that there is an emotional basis to what is happening, and it is most likely a negative one.

"Why is there water running from your eyes?" is the Martian view, which does not assume anything more than what is being observed.

In the Martian point of view, all possible explanations are up for consideration. The Martian might learn about human physiology—if the person is ill, has an allergy, or has something wrong with a contact lens that causes irritation. He keys in on psychology, finding that the person might be overwhelmingly emotional—either happy or sad—and the emotion "leaks out" in the form of tears. But here's the most important thing: our little Outer Space being has left room for every potential answer; thereby, entertaining as many positive possibilities as negative. And he is guaranteed to learn something either way.

About The Self-Development Project

The Self-Development Project and its peripherals have been structured to support your "inner Martian" by encouraging you to use what you read in the way that suits your needs best. I'll make suggestions, but they are just that—a suggested road to self-study. If there is any other underlying purpose, it's to teach you how to play again without worrying about The Rules, right or wrong answers, or matching up your findings with anyone else's.

The Self-Development Project is all about how you Can't Get It Wrong. By picking up this book and reading this far, you've already shown up for Day One of The Life You Want class. You are standing right here with me. You have everything you need to make the changes you seek, to embrace the things you want to keep, and to have a ridiculously good time—without checking to see if it's all right with the Professor (that's me).

You get an A for showing up. Simple as that. Because showing up means you will have picked up what you needed to learn to go out in the world and figure out your own answers to the exam—which will always be the right ones.

The Self-Development Project is a series of three books: *Volume I: Clean Out Your LifeCloset, Volume II: The Big Reboot,* and *Volume III: Be Your Own Masterpiece.* This handy little trilogy will partner with you in totally turning your life inside out and upside down until you've got an entirely self-created life.

Think of this series as the literary equivalent of that big mural of paper. We encourage you to draw the Ultimate You with a huge box of crayons, a batch of finger paints, glue and scissors, and sparkly bits—whatever takes your fancy!

What You'll Learn in Volume I: Clean Out Your LifeCloset

This first installment of *The Self-Development Project* consists of a total of sixteen chapters organized into four sections as follows:

Part I: Getting Clear.

If you are standing in the middle of a maelstrom (think teenager's bedroom), you have to get clear on what is currently in disarray. Focusing your telescope is how you set yourself up for that clarity. You'll take a closer look at places in your life that are like a three-legged stool—if any one of them is wobbly, you fall down. *Getting Clear On Your Purpose* helps you figure out what you're doing here. *Getting Clear In Your Relationships* helps you get the most out of your interactions with people around you. *Getting Clear With Spirit* helps you keep all the parts of your life in perspective.

Part II: Simplicity and Living Well With Less.

As you're cleaning up that proverbial bedroom, you will have detritus to clear out and duplicates to toss—some of the belongings may even be unrecognizable underneath all the dust and grime. It's the same way with life. I'll encourage you to look at life as a Tiny House—the idea that you have core essentials worth keeping, allowing everything else to be up for discussion. You'll find out how happy you can be with what you have, not what you *think* you *need*. You'll discover the delicious value of experiences rather than "Stuff." And you'll put on your practical thinking cap deciding which items to keep or toss out to simplify your existence.

Part III: Going With the Flow, Learning To Adapt.

Going with the flow is one of the easiest ways to open up your life. We're going to turn the idea of perfection on its ear. You'll learn why perfection isn't what you think it is, and that you have more of it than you realize. You'll find out that stumbling toward enlightenment is valuable. You'll examine those times when perfect destroys good. And because exceptions prove the rule, you'll discover when it's perfect to stand your ground or when saying "No" is a fabulous idea.

Part IV:
Stress Is a Complicated Friend.

This section covers that inevitable in-your-face companion of 21st-century humans. Not all stress is inevitably bad. We'll talk about the difference between good stress and bad stress. You'll learn how to listen to its messages: recognizing when stress is a warning sign, when it's like a hot water tap you can shut off with a little nudge, or when it's that freight train of "Are you kidding me?!" barreling down the tracks and needing your immediate attention.

The Adventure Pages.

You'll notice that at the end of each chapter, there are Adventure Pages. These pages are where my book becomes *our* book—yours and mine. You'll answer some questions to help you reflect on what you've read. You'll come up with places in your life where these ideas will work. You'll get to decide what your personal takeaways are (we call that "putting arrows in your quiver"). And you have space to write down what you believe to be the Most Important Piece of Knowledge you've gained. We'll encourage your inner artist to create a picture of what you've learned from every chapter along the way—making *Clean Out Your LifeCloset* into your own personal divination deck.

Playing with the Adventure Pages will enable you to see how my ideas can work for you. They highlight the parts of your life where you want deep change. They allow you to find your own way of phrasing things. And, I hope, they coax your Little Kid side to come out and play.

Part I:
Getting Clear

The Joy of a Clear Telescope

From the massive Keck structures on Hawaii's Mauna Kea to the simple ones that dot backyards on cloudless nights, telescopes transform hazy vistas into brilliant clarity. Viewing a distant star can activate wonder, a desire for adventure, and a profound sense of the vastness of the universe. But no matter what such breathtaking vistas trigger, our newfound clarity changes our worldview.

Like those stars powdering the skies, our lives are full of dreams, projects, plans, and ambitions. We can work on prioritizing our heart's desires. We can figure out how to give ourselves enough time to do them. We can let go of other people's dreams for us that have nothing to do with who we really are. Most importantly, we can decide what is essential for us in the long run.

Once we've acknowledged the goals and dreams we want in our life, we may still be left with a hazy mass of possibilities.

How do you pick a focus? Must you choose one dream out of many? Can your different goals support one another, or do you have one overriding desire?

How do you bring the thing you want most in the world into dazzling clarity?

Let's look at some helpful tips to keep your internal telescope sharp and focused.

Decide To Use Your Telescope

Your first step is to decide that gaining clarity is a priority. As Ralph Blum wisely says in *The Book of Runes*, "...even more than we are doers, we are deciders. And once the decision is clear, the doing becomes effortless."

The decision to seek clarity is, in itself, an action that will bring forward motion and excitement to the process of getting clear.

Clean the Lens

No matter how beautiful the view is outside, you'll never see it through a dirty window. That's why we have spring cleaning, to scrub away the winter gunge that's built up during those months of hibernating. A little spring cleaning of our internal telescope can get the glass sparkling and the vista sharp and enticing.

But what happens when the lens of your internal telescope continues to film over with daily diversions? Such deflections can be many and varied—and they take away from what's important. You may feel pressure from the urgent things that clamor for immediate attention: *Do the laundry! Run the errands! Play with the cat!* You can be seduced by the mindless things that are easy distractions: internet surfing, television, video games, and texting. You might feel emotionally entangled with someone else's situation, pulling you away from your own state of affairs.

All of these detours get in the way of accomplishing what truly matters to you: writing that article, planning a family night, exercising, meditating. When you look at all of the time-wasters and distractions, you'll come to realize you can set them aside—but that will require you to focus your telescope.

Focus Your Telescope

The world today provides us with more information than we can possibly process. If we fail to set limits or boundaries on where we focus our attention, we fall into a numb, drifting mind-state—never knowing where to rest and always feeling overwhelmed. Rather than settling for mindlessness, seek mindfulness.

Mindfulness is magic. When we are mindful, we pay attention to our life. The present moment is very much alive, yet we look at what is going on—both in and around us—without an emotional charge. Being mindful means we are actively making choices about our precious time and mind-space. When we use mindfulness to focus, clarity is the result. With clarity, you can "aim your arrow true." You will be able to identify a distraction quickly and find it easier to set it aside. You will catch yourself when you're thinking self-defeating thoughts and bring yourself back to productive mind-talk.

Pay attention to those times you find yourself thinking, *I can't do this.* Notice when you habitually berate yourself, compare yourself to others, or bemoan your current circumstances. These destructive thoughts and self-beliefs are the film and dirt on your internal telescope lens.

When you notice such self-talk, it's time to change perspective. Choose to think differently. Compassionately remind yourself of what you want. Is it possible for you to get it, do it, or make it happen? Yes, yes and yes! Be gentle with yourself as you go through these changes. Your mind is like a puppy; whapping it on the nose with a newspaper will not get you the outcome you want. You'll need time, repetition, and discipline to create a new habit with this mindfulness. Think of it as leash training your puppy, with treats at the end!

Aim Your Telescope

Meditation will keep your internal telescope from wobbling on its base. Too many people think meditation means sitting on a zafu cushion for hours at a time striving for no-mind. Think of meditation more as a calming of the chatter. Find time—as little as ten minutes a day—to sit quietly. Let your mind go softly silent. Coax your mental squirrels off their squeaky wheels for a while.

As your mind stills, those *urgent* beasties tend to go and sit in a corner. What you want to focus on quietly comes to sit with you. When it does, you can truly examine this most important companion and its friends, so you (and they) can work together most efficiently.

Meditation brings serenity, consolidating your energy for optimal use. The calming of the mind is one of the most powerful calibration tools your internal telescope can employ. The more you practice meditation, the more easily your mind will come into alignment.

Adjust the Lens

The beneficial structure of both you and your surroundings is crucial for clarity. Your body is the housing for your telescope. If your body isn't in sound working order, then neither are you.

These are nine simple ways to adjust your internal lens.

Cultivate simple, good habits. Get enough sleep. Eat good food at the right time, your attention centered on the meal. Avoid haphazardly shoving food in your body while on the go. Exercise to remind your body that you are partners in this adventure, which is good for raising your endorphin level.

Keep yourself and your surroundings clean and comfortable. When you're neither distracted by clutter nor feeling scruffy, focus is easier to come by.

Get dressed every day. Working in pajamas may sound lovely, but if not getting dressed dulls your clarity and confidence, the comfort isn't worth the trade-off.

Turn off the techno-tempters when you need to stay focused. According to Timothy Egan, contributing writer for The New York Times, a survey of Canadian media consumption by Microsoft concluded that a person's average attention span had fallen to eight seconds—down from 12 seconds in the year 2000. We now have a shorter attention span than goldfish. Why? Because our attention span shortens the more we indulge in electronics.

Set your schedule and keep your lists. Sheer willpower may not be enough to keep you on track, especially if you have numerous distractions throughout the day. Following a schedule and prioritizing items on a list helps to keep you focused.

Learn from other people with focused telescopes. The Law of Attraction states, "where your attention goes, so goes your existence." If you want clarity, then surround yourself with people and things that will cultivate clarity—not dissipate it.

Stay away from people who live in Never-land. Avoid people whose lives are filled with "no," "not," and "never," who make promises but never keep them, and who are habitually late. Eschew the company of the drifters who have no direction. They exhaust your energy with unproductive talk about dreams they'll never pursue because they're unwilling to do the work.

Find your tribe. Your true tribe is comprised of those who are excited by life, whose direction and purpose are at the tip of their tongues, and whose lives reflect their goals and desires with promise and effort combined.

Avoid the gloom-and-doom in the world. The adage in broadcasting is "If it bleeds, it leads." That kind of outlook is the last thing you need around you! Make an effort to find positive stories and inspirational books and podcasts. Listen to the words and ideas of those whose clarity of purpose and spirit has brought them joy and success. If they can achieve a happier state of being as they reach for their dreams, so can you.

Now that you have your telescope cleaned, set up, and aimed at the stars, the future is a lot clearer. Whether you choose to focus on your purpose, your relationship, or your spiritual growth, it's no longer a bunch of twinkly smudges above your head. There are vast galaxies of possibility—and they're yours to discover.

The Adventure Pages:

The Joy of a Clear Telescope

What was your personal definition of "Clarity" before you read this chapter? Any changes?

being able think or see things clearly. No obstruction

Have you been able to find Clarity on your own? How?

By focusing on the purpose or why for things.

What ideas in this chapter went *PING!* for you?

Excersize = mind/body Connection

Meditation

Mindfulness

technology takes you away from what matters

Any idea where you'd like to aim that telescope?

family and my own business of some type.

Put more arrows in your quiver: What three things do you want to take from this chapter and put to use in your life *right now*?

① You deserve to exercise

② ↓ social media. Who cares what anyone else is doing. This is your race

③ medidate - your mind loves you for it!

Here's your Invention Page!

Write down those three arrows on the blank page below. Draw, collage, or otherwise illustrate what your personal "Joy of a Clear Telescope card" would look like.

Getting Clear On Your Purpose

I've been doing intuitive work professionally since 1994 and full time since 2002. I've counseled thousands of clients over the years and in those sessions I've had questions come up that I'm happy to handle.

Here are a few examples of appropriate questions to ask an intuitive counselor:

"What do I need to know about my relationship?"
"How can I make my business thrive?"
"What will my finances look like over the next year?"
"Who are my guides?"
"Does my obsession or phobia have anything to do with a past life?"

Finding answers to such questions are all part and parcel of a good intuitive's repertoire. But there is one question I've gotten countless times and always *refuse* to answer: "What is my purpose?"

Would you go to your first Russian Literature class and tell your professor, "I know I'm supposed to read *War and Peace*, but why don't you just give me your Cliff notes and all the answers to the midterm?" Asking a psychic to tell you your purpose is like trying to get your hands on the teacher's manual to ace the test. What have you learned when you are handed all the answers without exploration? Zip, zilch, nada.

There are no shortcuts to discovering your purpose.

Your purpose and the Sentence of Passion that frames it form your rallying cry. They are the vapor trail you leave behind you in every encounter. When you go skidding into Heaven—on bald tires and fumes in your gas tank—what will you say to God when he hands you a drink (beer, tea, Red Bull) and says, "So tell me how it was down there?" At that moment, your life of passion and purpose is what you'll gleefully hold up in both hands, declaring, "Wow! Let me tell you all about it!"

Your purpose has to engage your passion. Your purpose is what you look forward to every morning. Your purpose is that soul-satisfying companion that sits with you every night and says, "We had fun today, didn't we?"

So why can't someone tell you who (or what) that companion is? Because no one else has lived your life, developed your interests, walked through your challenges, or pondered your questions. No one else can know the pattern of your existence. No one else knows your dreams and fears. It is these unique experiences that make up your *raison d'etre*.

How do you find your purpose? Examine your life, and ask yourself the following questions.

What has my life been about?

We all come into this world with themes, and specific paths and challenges. When we sketch out our blueprint in our pre-birth planning session, we know there will be lessons and roads that come to us in periodic waves. How we handle them determines how we succeed or fail.

Here are some examples:

If you have always had a roller-coaster relationship with money, how has that shaped your idea of prosperity? Do you feel you are doomed to a marginal existence? Does it make you want to make money no matter what? Does it inspire you to live more simply, so the feeling that was once one of lack now transforms into having enough?

If you are always the one who stands up for the underdog—whether or not you win—how does justice look to you? How do you want to bring it about on a daily basis?

If you consistently get overlooked for awards, disqualified in contests for odd reasons, or feel cheated out of your just due, does that make you bitter or better at being self-empowered?

If alcoholics and drug users surround you—yet you remain untainted—what does that tell you about your strength of will? How do you feel about those who use? Are you holier-than-thou? Do you wish you could help them get clean? Or do you ignore their existence?

Where does my happiness live?

To answer this question, let yourself relive your happiest moments. Think about the folks you admire and want to emulate. Give yourself time to think about what is truly good in your life. Some people may think of things or events. Others may think of people and structures. When you recognize how you "shape your happy," that will give you some definite ideas about how to engage your purpose.

It's also important to examine how you take care of yourself and others from day to day. Do you put yourself first? How do you like to gift people—with your time, a sentimental gesture, or simply an object? When do *you* feel valued? When do *you* feel taken for granted? Each answer will have a kernel of truth about who you are and what makes you tick.

Where do I find comfort?

We're not talking potato chips and video games here. Comfort means finding solace in things that bring you balance, joy, and stability.

I find joy in wordcrafting. When I can shape phrases, sentences, and paragraphs like so much brick and stone and steel, I get to create wonderful structures that move people's minds and hearts. I know I am centered and exactly where I need to be when I am with my words.

My friend Rina is a natural comedian. When she gets people laughing, whether it's at the water cooler or on a local stage, she's firing on all cylinders.

My beloved stepmother, Shirley, was never happier than when she was digging in the dirt, tenderly planting moss plugs under shady trees, and connecting with Nature down to her own roots.

We all took what comforted us and made it our purpose. As a teacher and intuitive, my words inspire and educate. Rina's comedy has made her a sought-after trainer helping people think outside the box at work. And Shirley went to college in her late 50s to get a degree in landscape architecture and work with nonprofit arboretums and conservatories. It's never too late to embrace your purpose.

If there are interests that always come forward no matter where you are, that is also a signal to you. Do you often donate your spare cash to an animal shelter? Are you always the first one volunteering for your public radio station's pledge drive? Do you look into the eyes of the homeless person on the corner after buying them a sandwich, and make a compassionate connection? These are all clues to the personal treasures that bring you comfort.

What crises changed my life?

Not everyone has experienced a seminal life-altering event, but if you have dealt with a crisis that was a serious turning point for you, mine the riches it contains. Living through a hurricane or tornado may remind you of the fragility of life and the importance of not wasting it. Responding to those caught in a major disaster (earthquake, rioting, warzones) may bring forward talents and strengths you didn't know you had. Think back on these situations: What marked your experience most strongly? What did you come away with regarding personal growth? If you faced a life-threatening illness and beat it, or survived a horrific accident, your will to live is worth examining and embracing.

How do I learn or work best?

This question is vital! Do you learn by seeing, hearing, or doing the thing? Are you a big-picture person or more detail-oriented? Are you more left-brained or right-brained? Do you run towards or away from change? Until you understand and use your best working methodologies, you may inadvertently short-circuit your purpose by trying to fit in into a life that can't succeed.

If you are right-brain dominant, your purpose will wither and die if you try to shoehorn it into a data-entry job. If you need stability and routine to feel centered and balanced, then a constantly changing job will exhaust you in short order. If you thrive best working with a team, then being cooped up in an office or working from home with no human contact for days at a time may not be your cup of tea. If you are a solo act, your best work occurs when you avoid structuring your purpose around people who want to give advice, provide input, or demand to be part of your process.

What do I want to be remembered for?

This last question is what sums up everything. We are all meant to leave this place better than we found it; the best way to do that is to pass on our purpose and passion in some form. When you imagine yourself gone from this body, and you're looking down from the Celestial Balcony, what do you want to see? Watching those people whose lives you've touched, what echoes of your teaching, inspiration, or knowledge do you want them to carry on? How is the world different for your passing through it?

For me, that question is answered simply but with great fervor: I want to inspire people to be more than they thought they could be. I want them to laugh when they remember how I taught them. If I can leave people with those gifts, I will have fulfilled my purpose with joy and satisfaction.

So how about you? Are you ready to get clear on your purpose, to carry it forward from today? If you answer these questions honestly and with careful consideration, your life's best companion will be standing in front of you—grinning with its suitcase packed and saying, "*Allons-y!* Let's get going!"

The Adventure Pages:

Getting Clear On Your Purpose

What did you think "Purpose" was before you read this chapter? Has the idea of Purpose changed for you?

Did you know what your Purpose was before you read this chapter? If so, what was it? Is it the same now?

What are you discovering about yourself as you ask the Six Questions of Purpose?

Who comes to mind when you think of someone who is very clear on their Purpose? Which of the questions we asked do you think they are clear on, and why?

Put more arrows in your quiver: What three things do you want to take from this chapter and put to use in your life right now?

Here's your Invention Page!

Write down those three arrows on the blank page below. Draw, collage, or otherwise illustrate what your personal "Clarity of Purpose card" would look like.

Getting Clear
In Your Relationships

Part of my daily work is being available on a large psychic website where people can call for a quick reading. I am a big believer in getting my client answers as fast as I can, and sometimes a question can be answered in just a few minutes. In those cases, it's better to use a per-minute go-between.

On that psychic website, 95 percent of my calls deal with relationships. The first—and sometimes only—question coming out of the phone is, "Can you tell me how so-and-so feels about me?" The question deals with someone the caller knows at work or someone they see but haven't yet connected with, and they hope to hear that there's a mutual interest. Other callers are post-break-up, and they want to find out if there is any hope of reconciliation.

I do my best to answer such questions, but I never fudge things. Most of the time, the lack of clarity between the person calling and the object of their affections is huge, and the disparity stares up from the cards in hard-to-miss vibrations. I tell callers what I see in the short amount of time we have together. But, if we had more time to delve into the situation, I would explain to them how to forge a good relationship—because making relationships last seems to be everybody's primary pitfall.

People often assume relationships refer to a romantic bond. Not even close! You have a relationship with every living creature on the planet: your husband, your mailman, your fur person, your tax accountant, the stranger behind you in line at Starbucks. When I talk about "getting clear in your relationships," it's more than just romance. Think of relationships as a garden. You've got to learn how to keep the flowers growing and the weeds from taking over so that the garden can flourish.

If time weren't an object in those "lightning reading" situations, I would give every client with a relationship question these eight points for making relationships last. Because they *work*.

Talk

You can't expect anyone—not even a psychic—to know what you want or what's bothering you if you never tell them. So many friendships and partnerships break up because too much goes unsaid for far too long, creating a rift that feels impossible to cross. If there is something amiss in a relationship or something is bothering you, and you don't understand why it's happening, then bring it up and put it on the table. It's essential; the only way to repair or redress the issue is to examine it.

When you feel talk is needed, tell the other person before the situation escalates. Make it clear, but work to keep the emotion out of the request. When two people go into a conversation as equals—rather than one making demands and one on the defensive—they can accomplish more understanding in less time with fewer bumps and bruises.

Make It About the Challenge, Not Personal Sniping

If something is bothering you or clouding a relationship, talk about the challenge.

Here's an example:

Let's say your partner is hogging all the closet space in your house or apartment. How would you typically handle this situation? If you say something to the effect of, "You always hog all the closet space and my stuff ends up on the floor," what kind of response would you expect to come next? I'd guess an unfavorable one. What if the statement was reframed as, "My clothing is ending up on the floor; can we figure out a way for me to have more closet space?" Notice, the "we" in that request pulls you and your partner together for a relationship-based solution. You won't come across as saying, "I think this is unfair" or "you are a closet pig."

Remember, when the talk is about the challenge and *not* the person, our partner's guard doesn't go up. When we feel included and not on the defense, we're more willing to listen and work on a compromise. A mutual challenge to solve is less provocative than a personal attack.

To vs. At

This simple grammatical rule is more important than people realize. When we yell *to* others because we're frustrated or angry, we are venting about something that may not have anything to do with them. All we want is for someone to hold space for us and validate our emotions through their compassionate attention.

When we yell *at* others, then they become the target. And if they can't distinguish between the two, more miscommunication is usually the result.

Jessica and her husband, Robert, run into this issue all the time. Robert is an art director for an advertising firm. It's a huge job with a lot of pressure and stress. He has to be very careful about what he says and to whom, which means a lot of his *stuff* gets bottled up and can only come out when he's away from the office. When Robert comes home from work, fuming and complaining, Jessica's first and most important question is, "Are you yelling *to* me or *at* me?" This question forestalls massive amounts of misdirected anger and unnecessary arguments. Jessica can listen carefully without worrying that Robert's anger and frustration are directed at her.

When you feel your temper or frustration rising, and there is someone within earshot, be clear about whether they are the cause—or your support system. If the individual is in the line of fire and not the intended target, stop. Take a deep breath. If all you need is to pop your cork or let loose the steam vent on your internal pressure cooker, tell them so first. Prepare your support team so they are ready to listen without needing to duck the fireworks. And if they *are* the target of your explosion? Remember, the idea is to explore a mutual challenge, not attack.

Fix vs. Listen

In any relationship, but most especially a partnered one, there's always a fixer. Fixers see or hear perceived problems and they immediately make suggestion after suggestion until they come up with a way to solve them. That becomes a problem when people are not asking for advice. Many people (myself included) just want to vent or think out loud to see if a solution makes sense. We crave a supportive sounding board, not someone else's two cents on a matter.

Claude and Michele got married in their 40s after both had been single for many years. At the beginning of their marriage, Michele would frequently interrupt Claude's musings: "Well, what about this?" or, "Have you thought about that?" These interruptions forced Claude to constantly defend his reasoning or decisions, which derailed his thinking process. Inevitably, Claude would end up exploding at Michele, furious at what he considered her "meddling." An argument would ensue, having nothing to do with Claude's initial situation.

After some serious dialogues, Michele has come to understand that if Claude is having an out-loud go-round about a problem or challenge, the magic phrase is, "Do you want me to try and fix this, or just listen?" If Claude wants her input, he invites Michele to help him solve the problem. If Claude says, "Please just listen," then Michele puts the Spiritual Duct Tape over her mouth and holds the space for Claude to figure things out.

Claude confesses feeling supported enormously

by this new action, and his "out-loud thinking" finds answers more quickly than it might have otherwise.

The 60-60

People talk about 50-50 relationships, but I believe in 60-60. It's the idea that every individual goes a little bit more than halfway to listen, appreciate, and engage with the other. The extra 10 percent tends to overlap and gives the relationship a strong anchor for the tough times.

To be honest, relationships of any kind are always in flux. There's never perfect equality. Sometimes one person will lean on the other a little more—needing more attention or help during a tough situation. That, my friends, is Life. If each partner is willing to give more on occasion or in the face of unforeseen circumstances, there is loving equilibrium. The leaned-on person knows that their own relationship reservoir has been filled in the past, and they have the emotional support to give now without feeling used.

When I had my third bout of cancer early in my marriage, Carle and I already had four years of a relationship and eighteen months of marriage behind us. We both understood the idea of 60-60 and had been building up that reservoir from our first date. As a result, Carle was able to be there for me under terribly difficult circumstances—ones that, for many other couples, spelled separation or divorce. Fourteen years later, that 60-60 means our marriage is stronger than ever.

The 60-60 is one of the best practices you can adopt to keep a relationship intact for the long run.

You First, Then the Relationship

"Wait, what about the 60-60?" you ask? Let's not confuse *you first* with, "It should be all about me!" The reality is simple: if you fail to take care of yourself first, you have nothing to give to anyone else.

Crystal is an acupuncturist who runs her own business. She is also the one who is always *there* for everybody. Frequently, she will change office hours to help out a friend. She'll put off her own self-care because her mother needs to talk. She'll do without an important purchase because her child needs money to go on a class trip. Eventually, Crystal begins to notice that her business has gone downhill because she has put everyone else first. But when she needs help, no one believes her. No one understands her emotional depletion because she has never asked anyone for anything before. Even people closest to her assume she's just having a bad day. As a result, she loses her business. Many of her relationships fall by the wayside because she has nothing left to give them—not the way they've come to expect.

Sometimes you are unable to move a work deadline. Sometimes someone is asking for a personal appointment that can derail your health and stable progress. And sometimes you simply need some time for yourself without demands. In all of these cases, don't say a "Yes" you don't mean. Learn when saying "No" is a fabulous idea. Most importantly, remove the guilt you attach to making yourself unavailable. Calmly making it clear that you are a priority too can help your friends, family, and partner accept that when you say "No," it's not a rejection, but a point of self-care.

Don't Sublimate Needs

Familiarity is comforting for most people, especially in relationships. But Life asks us to change and grow, and that can't help but affect our connections with others. In order to honor our authenticity within a relationship, we need to admit when changes are necessary. Otherwise, communication breakdowns and misunderstandings are sure to result.

Here's an example:

Serena and Minni have been friends for years. They have always met on Friday nights for drinks and dinner. But as they've gotten older, Serena has noticed that drinks and a late dinner leave her feeling battered around the edges the next day. Minni's constitution, on the other hand, is no different at 34 than it was at 24; she doesn't feel the effects of a party night at all.

Serena wants to be a *good* friend, so she never shares these feelings with Minni. Eventually, the Friday night meetup becomes so toxic for Serena that she begins making up excuses to bail on plans. Minni feels that Serena is no longer invested in the friendship, and the entire relationship cools. Within a year, they are no longer talking to each other, assuming that they have just "grown apart."

If Serena had told Minni honestly that Friday nights needed to change in some form—a different type of restaurant, an earlier meeting time—the friendship would likely be going strong. Remember the *Make It About the Challenge* rule? If a habitual part of the relationship needs changing or if your life has altered parts of the relationship's expectations, talk about it. Ignoring the changes or avoiding the conversation will always end up fueling a misunderstanding. The relationship will thank you in the long run if you both address what you want and need from each other.

Give the Relationship the Time It Requires

Just as we all need *me* time, relationships need *us* time. While some of us are incredibly lucky to have those friendships that last through long bouts of non-communication, most relationships need some proper care and feeding.

Our lives can become overfilled with work, media, and demands from every direction. The old idea of coming over for an evening or spending a day together doing an amiable bunch of nothing is hard to come by. And because our globe is shrinking—sometimes our best friends are in Nairobi when we live in Nevada—that can put a double strain on things because getting together physically these days is rare-to-impossible.

Make a conscious effort. Send an email or text (the relationship equivalent of MREs). Get on a phone call or Skype. Make time for a friendship to grow. If you're lucky enough to be within meeting distance, set aside time to be in each other's company. It's tempting to let "have to" get in the way of "want to," but any friendship worth keeping is worth cultivating (and maintaining a friendship is easier than looking for a new one).

As for a romantic relationship, my philosophy is always, "Friends before lovers, not lovers before friends." Why? When you are friends, you have built up some degree of trust and understanding of each other's foibles and world views. That level of confidence in each other makes the evolution to the physical part of the relationship sweeter and easier. Lovers before friends can create sticky situations where you're unsure about the person you woke up next to. You have no idea what they're thinking or how they are going to react. And later that afternoon is when you usually pick up the phone and call me, isn't it?

When a relationship—any relationship—is clear to both partners, the bond can grow strong and healthy roots. As any good gardener knows, the beauty of the blooming garden is worth every bit of effort and love you can lavish upon it. I encourage you to look at each of your relationships as a personal flower patch. Pull up the weeds. Feed and water your delicate flowers sufficiently. They'll repay you with heart's ease, nourishment, and beauty for a long time.

The Adventure Pages:

Getting Clear In Your Relationships

What are the toughest things about making good relationships for you?

How can what you read in this chapter help you change your relationships with others?

Turn this on its head! How can what you've read in this chapter help you have a better relationship with *yourself*?

Which relationship that you have *right now* would you like to try some of these new thoughts on? Why is that the relationship you chose? How might these new thoughts help?

Put more arrows in your quiver: What three things do you want to take from this chapter and put to use in your life right now?

Here's your Invention Page!

Write down those three arrows on the blank page below. Draw, collage, or otherwise illustrate what your personal "Getting Clear In Your Relationships card" would look like.

Getting Clear With Spirit

People ask me about clarity of Spirit all the time, but it's a difficult idea to grasp. I spoke with a fellow master intuitive. I called a Jesuit priest who is a close friend. I chatted with folks in the entrepreneurial community. I even sat with my own guides on the subject. Everybody I approached came up with a different answer.

Does that mean clarity of Spirit is unique to the individual? I think so. The difference is in the details.

Let's do a bit of defining first. When I mention *Spirit* in this context, I am not referring to "talking to the deceased." We're talking about how we plug into the Central Energy—God, Spirit, Source—however you are comfortable with describing it. When we can disentangle ourselves from the everyday morass of physical, mental and emotional demands—settling ourselves into the internal quiet, to set them aside—Spirit comes closer in a clearer fashion.

But what remains tricky is the *how* of finding clarity. And there are lots of different takes on *how* to search. My longtime friend Michael, the Jesuit priest, puts it this way to me, "The more I submit my life to the great mystery, to be loving, forgiving, generous, and challenging, the more I am able to do so. I learned the instructions by following a spiritual path. I paid attention to the way that the Divine manifested itself in the world, and then I started to do the same. Little by little."

"Is that the clarity of self?" I asked him. "Are you saying that the clearer you get on your *self*, the clearer your link to Spirit?"

Michael shook his head. "For me, at least, clarity of Spirit is often the opposite of clarity of self. The more I submit to the utter mysteriousness of it all, the better I can intuit the motions of the Divine. Sometimes I don't trust myself; I need to know which parts of myself to trust, and that requires me to lose myself first."

Strangely enough, part of the definition of clarity of Spirit is an oxymoron. The less I believe I have all the answers and open myself up to other ways of looking at the world, the more I find the underlying theme that runs through everything. For this reason, I completely understand where Michael is coming from.

A Gods' Eye View

Here's an exercise to try when you are feeling fogged in and unable to reach that clarity:

Imagine you are a hundred-foot-tall deity standing on top of a cliff. You look down upon a village. You watch it for a long time. You can see the births and the deaths, the marriages and the divorces, the alliances and the squabbles. But as you observe—because you are not in the midst of everything—you merely notice the patterns. You stay objective in your view.

Now, take whatever it is that's causing your mental fog and view it in the same detached way. Rise above the situation, above the emotions, above the worries, above the feelings of stress. What happens? Are you clearer? Do things settle down? What can you see that you missed before?

When we are not in the midst of our problems and challenges—but can step away (or step up) to view them from the outside—patterns and repeated behaviors become clearer. Our ways of self-sabotage stand out. And when we see what is keeping us from clarity, it is easier to remove it or walk around it to find our peaceful center.

Interestingly, every Tibetan Lamasery overlooks a village, bustling with life. Perhaps they, too, understand that being able to watch the world from a distance gives you a better sense of the whole, no?

Headspace vs. Heartspace

Another way I like to explain the journey to clarity is headspace versus heartspace. Our head speaks to us of logic—a cause-and-effect, tab-A-into-slot-B sort of existence. We demand answers. We need to understand everything. The more we try to figure something out, the less objective we are. Judgments, expectations, and assumptions all crowd in—arguing with and elbowing one another—and making no room for the tranquil space of Spirit that sits in a corner, watching and waiting for things to settle down.

Headspace versus heartspace also means that while religious texts of any flavor may help you understand your particular slant on the Source, it may not give you clarity of Spirit. All of these writings are somehow filtered through another human mind. As one of my fellow intuitives says, "Religious rules and strictures are someone's ego telling us what to do. Clarity of Spirit is the ability to see through the smoke and mirrors to pure essence." I agree. The Divine, the Source, presents Itself when we seek It from within. The Divine doesn't follow man-made rule books. It doesn't say "Yes" to Vijay and "No" to Maria and "Not yet" to Ahmed because of how they seek the One.

Spirit is open. Spirit is available. Spirit has no judgment.

I believe if you seek clarity of Spirit, it is likely to be found in silence. Set aside a time when you don't *have* to have the answers. You simply sit. This isn't mindfulness I'm talking about; you are not busy thinking about the present moment. Rather, you are floating. Give yourself permission to *not* know.

As the right and wrong of seeking Spirit diminishes, you will find yourself growing both calmer and lighter. The black and white of the world ceases to badger you from morning to night. There is compassion for all beings and an understanding that the reasons the world is the way it is don't need to be solved this minute.

What did my own guide, Baruchiel, have to say on the subject?

> *You will find clarity of Spirit when you acknowledge, accept and rejoice in the fact that you are not your body, not your mind, not your experiences. You are and always*

have been part of the Ineffable Whole—unceasing, unchanging, non-judging. When you feel in balance and complete, when you feel that you are One with All That Is, there is clarity of Spirit.

Spirit in the human soul understands the impermanence of all. Because all things are coming to be and passing away, attention is placed on that which abides. That which abides in the human soul is formed of charity, compassion, love, and the understanding of the interconnection with all those sharing your reality.

So while many of these chapters are in a sense *how to* articles, this particular chapter focuses on *why to*. Why is clarity of Spirit important—a treasure?

To be blunt, you hurt less. You are kinder to yourself. Yes, it's important to have all that charity, compassion, love and understanding of our connectedness so you can reach out to others in the world. But we put ourselves last too often. We forgive everyone but ourselves. We are kind to others but chide ourselves for not doing or being enough.

Getting clear with Spirit means *you*, too. Especially you. Because the spirit that becomes clear is the one that resides inside you.

Today, set aside all your tasks. Stop trying to fix and improve yourself, or become a better person. Today, take a little time to connect with that which knows nothing is wrong with you, and nothing ever was. Sit with your Self. Let everything around you settle, the way a pool of water clears when the pebble sinks to the bottom. All you have to do is Be, and serenity settles within you. Clarity of Spirit is yours for the not-asking.

The Adventure Pages:

Getting Clear With Spirit

When you hear someone speak about "Spirit," what does your version of Spirit look like to you?

What part does Spirit play in your life? Is it enough for you, or are you seeking a greater connection?

Think of a recent time when you were stressed and unable to get out of your own way—unable to connect with Spirit in a manner that could nourish you. Try the "deity on the mountain" exercise. How different would things be if you'd climbed that mountain?

Put more arrows in your quiver: What three things do you want to take from this chapter and put to use in your life *right now?*

Here's your Invention Page!

Write down those three arrows on the blank page below. Draw, collage, or otherwise illustrate what your personal "Getting Clear with Spirit card" would look like.

Part II: Simplicity and Living Well With Less

Life As a Tiny House

These days, people have houses that are too big for them. But it hasn't always been that way. I asked my friend, Julie Alibrando, what she knew about the trends since she's been in residential home sales for decades. Julie is a seasoned realtor in the Midwest market, and she agreed that buyers' expectations have grown by leaps and bounds.

"There's really no such thing as a 'starter' home any longer. First time home buyers are looking for a home that's as big as or bigger than the home their parents waited 10 or 15 years to purchase. Families are getting smaller, but the homes they want keep getting bigger!"

Julie shook her head, marveling. "Most of our buyers are requesting three to four bedrooms, an office, three bathrooms, a finished lower level, and three-car garages. Yet these requests come from a family size of either two adults only or adults with one to two children."

Because of the siren call of consumerism and the desire to keep up with the Joneses, people buy big houses and fill them with more stuff than they can possibly use—throwing things away when they become the least bit shabby, old-fashioned, or no longer trendy.

To feed that voracious beast of More, people work longer hours and become more stressed. They try to shoehorn in everything they feel *must* get done: attending sports practices to make sure their children are considered good enough, saying "Yes" to friends to avoid looking bad or mean, getting all the chores done. Forget having time for pleasurable or healthy activities like exercise or the calming downtime it takes to live in this world of 24/7 demands.

Is it any wonder that 35 million Americans—over 16 percent of our entire population—are so depressed that they need treatment, whether or not they can afford it?

Enter the Tiny House Movement and the craving for simplicity. The Tiny House Movement is a social swing toward houses that are multi-purpose, without an inch of wasted space. In a house no bigger than 400 square feet (and often "off the grid"), people get down to the necessities. They turn away from the insistent gotta-have-gotta-do-gotta-look-like-money mantra that modern life keeps whispering in our ears. At the same time, people who make the decision to downsize drastically in this manner often find themselves having *more* of what they actually want: more time, more ease, and more concentration in their lives.

Tiny House Living doesn't mean deprivation; it means seriously thinking about what matters most to you and ditching all but those few priorities. Small as it is, a well-designed and well-thought-out Tiny House has a better living quality than larger houses so crammed with Stuff that people ricochet from one thing to another—unable to feel settled or think clearly.

The Stuff Experiment

If you look at your life as your House, do you fill it with so much Stuff you can't move? How much of your life do you focus on impressing others? How much of your life do you live in a scarcity mindset? How much of your life are you keeping up to a certain standard because everybody is doing it?

Try an experiment with me:

- [ ] Find twenty objects in your house that mean something to you or you think you can't live without. They can be pictures, tools, gadgets, knick-knacks, anything you choose.

- [ ] Put them all on a table.

- [ ] Take a look at these items for thirty seconds.

- [ ] Then walk out of the room.

- [ ] Now, try to list everything that you put on the table.

How did you do? Most people are unable to list all of the objects. They feel stressed even trying. Were you able to immediately recall the good feelings you got when you bought, used, or had an experience with any of the items? I'm willing to wager that you had a hard time even remembering when or why you purchased the majority of what's on the table.

Now, here's Part Two of the experiment.

- [ ] This time, choose only five out of the twenty objects and put the rest away.

- [ ] Look at the five items for thirty seconds.
- [ ] Then walk out of the room.
- [ ] List everything you kept on the table.

You were able to list the entire group, correct? And, you were probably able to remember the whens and whys of each item, right?

What you did in this experiment is what we call simplifying. Instead of trying to hold onto more things than we can possibly manage, we are able to concentrate on what we love, what we use, and what benefits us.

How do you live more with less? Now that you understand the Tiny House Living concept, you can start simplifying your life today without even moving from where you currently live by asking yourself these questions.

If I had a year to live, what would be important to me?

When we are unconscious of how time is passing, we feel we can make time and room for everything. If you can imagine your life as ending a year from today, it's an excellent way to focus on the things that matter to you and to see what has taken up space in your life that you could well do without.

What do I find myself doing or using most often?

There are certain things we do, use or experience that are core to who we are and what we want out of life. For me, it's the simple things. My Tarot deck gets used a dozen times a day for my clients and my own self-examination. My well-seasoned frying pan comes out every morning to make Carle's fried eggs and to do most of my sautéing tasks during the day. My softest pair of Yoga pants and my most comfortable shirts continually cycle in and out of the laundry. When you list your "everyday favorites," you may be surprised to find out how small their number is.

What do I surround myself with that has ceased to matter?

Are there books you no longer read that still take up shelf space? What about the friendships that are more high maintenance than nurturing? Are you in a habitual thought pattern that reflects outmoded beliefs or ideas that now do more harm than good? When we recognize that parts of our life are obsolete, they are easier to put in the "done with" pile to make room for what matters today.

What have I gone unconscious about?

Do a little exploring. How many things in your kitchen have you overbought because you forgot you had them? How many articles of clothing have you purchased because they beckoned to you at the time but you've never worn them?

Look at your bank account. How many online impulse buys have you made (online games, cool doo-dads and gadgets, website subscriptions) that you can't recall? Even more, how many times have you used those items? Do you even remember how many online subscription sites you belong to or how often they automatically renew?

Consciousness around our virtual "dragon hoards" will show us just how many true treasures we have in our pile of Stuff—and how much of it is mere throwaway trash and costume jewelry.

What benefits other people in the house, not just me?

If you live with others, does everybody have their own Stuff that overlaps? Do you have duplicate items that you could consolidate into one? Does everyone in your home understand the value of sharing and simplifying? Or, does everybody in the house insist on having the same objects just for themselves?

While everyone needs their own toothbrush, they may not *all* need their own copies of *Harry Potter*.

What intangible clutter do I have?

Intangible clutter is made up of the tasks, relationships, obligations and emotions that waste your time. They don't feed your soul. They don't give you any benefit. And, they hip-check out of the way other things that would be more important, valuable, and fulfilling.

When you sit down and honestly ask yourself these questions, you may be astonished at how much you have in your life that you neither need nor want.

How To Start Simplifying

When I started researching the topic of simplifying, I found over 100 suggestions that could help us change how we view *having*. But that's far more information than you need right now (simplify, remember?). I pared down the list to ten ideas that can start moving your life in a Tiny House direction.

1. **Be conscious.** Doing things automatically or without thinking is the cause of more clutter than you can imagine. Look at anything you are considering buying and ask yourself, *Can I live without it?* Look at every relationship and notice, *Does this relationship support me, drain me, or provide balanced energy for me?* Look at your habitual thoughts and decide, *Are they true for me? Are they useful? Are they healing?*

2. **Detach your identity from your belongings.** We are not our jobs, our family titles, our sports teams, our new car, our bells-and-whistles computer, or our name-brand clothes. These material items do not determine what we are worth! When you accept that you are not defined by what you own, getting rid of them (and not buying more) will be infinitely easier.

3. **Eat slowly, without distractions.** It's a small change, but enjoying our food is such an important lesson in teaching ourselves what "enough" is! Savor what you have. Be conscious of what you put in your mouth without the distraction of a book, television, or other sensory diversions. When we are aware of what we are eating and how much we are enjoying it, we eat less.

4. **Evaluate commitments and time-takers.** There are so many tasks we've done for years, prom-

ises we made long ago where both parties have forgotten why we made them, and routines so ingrained in our schedules that we're not even aware we're doing them. Look at anything that requires your participation. Ask yourself if it moves you forward or nourishes you in any way. If volunteering at the local animal shelter or being a Big Brother or Big Sister nourishes you, as well as those you help, then keep it on your list. But if what you're examining no longer serves you, put it in the "dump" pile.

5. **Go for quality, not quantity.** I learned this one from my frugal-by-nature husband. If we have a large purchase to make (a new refrigerator, a lawn tractor, a car) we spend time weighing our options, looking at consumer ratings, and finding out where we can get the best deal. Then we buy the best we can afford and it lasts for a long time. Try paying that kind of attention to smaller purchases. Two kitchen gadgets may be on the shelf, and the lesser one may be on sale. But if you have to buy three of them in the span of two years, they are no bargain if the other slightly pricier gadget gives you years of service. In that case, paying more up front may be better in the long run.

6. **Limit your media consumption.** In our household, we automatically mute every single pharmaceutical commercial. Why? We don't want to hear about diseases we don't have or need to think about. Every other commercial is about the diabetes we are sure to develop or the heart attack waiting for us around the corner. Even normal body glitches are

now touted as diseases if it will sell another drug ("Did you know you could have usedtobenormalitis or UTBNI? Ask your doctor if Fixituban is right for you!"). The fears these commercials seek to instill in us lead us to pester our doctors about yet another pill we would never have known about had Big Pharma not warned us we couldn't live without it. Advertising is advertising. We can live without 98 percent of what they promote, but marketing folks are good at seducing you without your being aware of it. The less you let advertising enter your consciousness, the less you will want. It's that simple.

7. **Redefine the concept of enough.** The best example of not understanding *enough* comes from my grandmother's ideas on food: "Eat one more bite than you want. Then you've had enough." How many pairs of shoes is enough? How many boxes of pasta is enough? How much vacation is enough? How much self-time is enough? How many obligations are enough? Be conscious when it comes to what enough is. Your version may differ from someone else's, but that's okay. The only one who has a say in what enough means for you is you.

8. **Reduce, Reuse, Recycle.** We're not talking about hoarding everything just in case you need to use it later. However, it pays to remember the maxim from the Depression, "Use it up, wear it out, make it do or do without." Figure out how you can consolidate several things into one. Find ways to turn one no-longer-used thing into a new wow-this-is-useful thing. Take the time to separate out plastics

and cardboard and get them to the recycling plant. Wade through your clothes, the kids' toys, and anything else of which you have multiples and get them to a second-hand center so others who have less can find and cherish them.

9. **Simplify your wardrobe.** This tip is both hard and easy. Hard because we all have pieces we love that we only get to wear occasionally—or pull out on a special occasion to match that perfect, but rarely-donned item. We all know that when we have multiples of *anything*, some of them never get used. Try the old hanger-reversal trick: Put all your hangers backward on the bar. When you wear something, put the hanger back on the bar the way you would normally. After six months or a year, look at all the hangers that are still backward on the bar. Notice what never got worn. Do you really need it? Do you still love it? If not, out it goes. Do the same for shoes, jewelry, and anything clothing-related. Find a way to see what you are and are not using. If you don't use it, send it off to someone who will.

10. **Stop worrying about norms or what is expected of you.** The biggest advice is saved for last. So much of what we have or what we do has been dictated by what others think we should have or do—or even be. When you let go of listening to others' judgments of you and what you surround yourself with, you will find it wonderfully easy to slow down consumption. You'll be able to pare Stuff down to what you really love. You'll stop looking over your shoulder for validation. Wayne

Dyer said it best: "What other people think of me is none of my business."

Finally, remember this question: Who lives in your tiny, beloved Life house? *You* do. The house of your life is yours and yours alone, even if you choose to share parts of it with others. And you just might find that living in a Life house that's smaller than you've experienced opens you up to a great big life in general.

The Adventure Pages:

Life As a Tiny House

How do you view "Stuff?" How do you view your Stuff in particular?

How does your Stuff serve you? Is there Stuff that now merely gets in the way? If so, what specific Stuff is it and how does it hinder you?

Which of the "Six Questions About Stuff" gave you the most insight on your Stuff Situation?

Put more arrows in your quiver: What three things do you want to take from this chapter and put to use in your life right now?

Here's your Invention Page!

Write down those three arrows on the blank page below. Draw, collage, or otherwise illustrate what your personal "Life As a Tiny House card" would look like.

Finding Happiness With What You Have Right Now

I really do love to play with food. Puttering in the kitchen is a wonderful form of therapy for me, and it results in a freezer full of home cooking for nights when I'm on the road and Carle has to eat solo—or when my schedule's too full to make something fresh for dinner.

In my kitchen, you may not recognize some of the names on the containers. That's because I can't resist a good pun. For instance, chicken cacciatore is labeled "Patriotic Chicken" (Chicken Catch a Tory, for you Revolutionary War buffs). But it also signals my skill with invention. More than once, I've had containers labeled beef, chicken or pork "TR." TR, in this case, stands for Teddy Roosevelt and his famous quote, "Do what you can, with what you have, where you are." These labels recognize that what's inside is more than likely a one-time recipe because I had to substitute, combine ideas, or otherwise make do with what we had in the pantry and refrigerator. And when I serve up a batch of TR, I've never yet had Carle do anything but smile blissfully and ask for seconds.

Let's compare my TR adventures with the experience of someone who thinks that a recipe has to be followed precisely. For this person, it may induce stress (*What if I get it wrong? What if people say they don't like it because it doesn't taste like it's supposed to?*). The uncompromising recipe follower may also make extra trips to the grocery store if they're missing an ingredient—sticking so stringently to the rules that cooking becomes less about creativity and more of a chore.

Now, expand that idea. If your house and your life are your virtual pantry, can you learn to make a wonderful life with what you've got? Or are you going to fret constantly that you don't have what everyone else deems the right ingredients to be happy, successful, or *all that*? When we are too busy looking at what we don't have—what we think we need for everything to be okay—we're not living in the moment. We're looking to the future where all those goodies might be hiding. When we think about "not having" (whether it's what we are missing right now, what we never had before, or what we might not have in the future) we're stuck in a place we can never change. No matter how you look at it, "not having" equals bad with that kind of mindset.

How about appreciating all that you have right now? Or where you are? If I were going to give you a recipe for "Happiness TR," it would go something like this:

Be in the moment

Attitude of gratitude

Martian curiosity

No rules just right

Thinking outside the box

Not attached to outcomes

Be In the Moment

When you are in the moment, you are not thinking about past and future. You are completely alive to your surroundings, your senses, and your thought processes. No use in thinking about what *used to* be in your pantry or what you're *going to* buy next week. What do you have *right now*?

Making a list of what we have in the pantry can help to stimulate some great ideas. Take a little time to jot down what you see in front of you: current ideas, physical supplies, reference resources, spiritual senses, even how you are feeling emotionally at the moment. When we are acutely aware and appreciative of where we are and what we have, we will boost our creativity to its peak performance.

Attitude Of Gratitude

Our intentions and attitudes are our vibration. Gratitude is just about the most positive vibration you can have. After all, like begets like. When you feel gratitude for whatever you have, you get more. When you are sulking because you do not have something, you see yourself as *not* having; and what you get is more of that—*not* having.

What is your attitude when you sit to a meal? Are you grateful to have food, sitting and savoring it? Or, are you grumbling and shoving it down almost faster than you can taste it? Since our body systems work more efficiently without stress, we gain more nourishment from food when we're eating with an attitude of gratitude.

We can say the same about life. When you are grateful for what you have, rather than seeing it as lesser than or inferior to, you enjoy life more. An enjoyable life will do more for you, and will serve you far better than grudgingly viewing it as "making do."

I'm grateful for a hot shower. Grateful for the loony pile of fur-and-purr that wakes me up every morning. Grateful that my brain still works and I can still write my books. Grateful for a partner that supports my work. Even the smallest ingredient can be fabulous in whipping up a dish of Happy on a daily basis.

What are you grateful for?

Martian Curiosity

Martian Curiosity is one of my favorite ingredients in the Happiness pantry.

Go back to one of the first ideas we introduced you to in the book: pretend that that you are from an entirely different planet and look at everything around you with delighted inquisitiveness. When we have absolutely no preconceived notions about an event, a situation, or where we are in life at the moment, we are truly limitless. My friend Meg, when she could not decide what to do for dinner, would chop up onions, throw in some garlic, and sauté them in butter and olive oil. She would sniff the air until the mélange of ingredients told her how they should taste together that day. She conversed with her ingredients each evening for a month. As a result, she discovered thirty different (and delicious) recipes to try.

Life is full of those mysterious fragments, waiting to form something wonderful. When we have a situation—luck or challenge, opportunity or setback, a party or solitude, a work day full of progress or a day with writer's block—we must play with what it contains. Stir those elements around in your mental pan and take in a good whiff. What do they remind you of? What do you want to do with these ingredients to make them nourishing?

Who knows? You could end up with a recipe for sugar-coated chocolate-covered pizza pickle bites—and it just might be the Next Big Thing (because only a Martian attitude could conjure up such a recipe).

No Rules, Just Right

The slogan from Outback Steakhouse™, *"No Rules, Just Right,"* makes a heck of a lot of sense when you are using what ingredients you have in your Happiness pantry.

Two brilliant examples of this attitude are Stephen Hawking and the late Roger Ebert. Both men were afflicted with some pretty horrendous health challenges: Hawking with ALS, and Ebert with recurring jaw cancer, which eventually took his voice from him. Neither person wasted time bemoaning their fate. Hawking is still the preeminent scientific mind in the world today, making one discovery after another that can change the fate of mankind. And Ebert attended movie screenings, wrote reviews, and managed to stay close to his wide circle of friends and colleagues—his loving wife with him—until the day he died.

You do not *need* health and wealth, marriage and success, and a house and minivan (or a Porsche) to have the Happy Life. There are no rules about what being happy means, how happy you should be, or how much happiness you should have at any given time. My 847 square foot house is enough. We'll never be upside down on our mortgage. We have a gorgeous mountain view. And I'm surrounded by blissful tranquility. Having grown up in a wealthy New Jersey suburb, *this* life—believe me—is not what I expected happiness to resemble in my sixties. But it does. Absolutely and without question.

No rules. Just right. And for me, it certainly is.

Thinking Outside the Box

I often say to my clients, "Let's not only think outside the box but also outside the room where the box is stored." The wilder a concept, the better when it comes to cultivating happiness in unexpected places.

A longtime friend of mine lives with a tent, her dog, her kitchen utensils, and a few supplies. She has gone from Massachusetts to Maine to Georgia in three years. She sometimes lives out of her car, and sometimes out of her tent. She has discovered that being footloose and fancy-free—without the responsibilities of a home, a mortgage, a job, or a landlord—is exactly what she wants in life. Some people would call her homeless. She never thinks that way; instead, she cheerfully refers to herself as "merely unhoused." She has exactly the life she wants and feels not one whit sorry for herself. For her, happiness is outside of needing the comfort of having a roof over one's head.

By thinking outside the box and deciding not to live by standardized, conventional rules, my friend has found a rare peace and happiness. And I say bravo to her for knowing herself so well.

Not Attached To Outcomes

When you are not attached to completing something in a certain way, anything can be joyful. In my kitchen adventures, I've baked bread that hasn't risen. So I made bread pudding. I've created casseroles that looked odd. So I added cheese and breadcrumbs on top and labeled them "Dodo Surprise," defined as "this puppy will be extinct, and probably for a good reason, but we'll have it for tonight." I've had wines that turned. So I made vinegar for my dressings.

Are there times we want our life to contain the perfect loaf of bread, the brilliant meal, and the fine wine? Of course. But there are also times when cherished plans go awry, a dinner party for twelve turns out to be for three because of the weather, or a business project absolutely deflates. When such things happen, see what you can do with the leftovers, the results, or the apparent failures to flip them to your advantage. Who knows? Perhaps you'll turn the hodgepodge into something unexpectedly fun and wonderful.

When you are ready to stop looking at what happiness *ought to be*, take a deeper look inside your virtual pantry. Rather than believing you don't have the right things to be happy right now, notice all the things you *do* have. The things you've taken for granted…the stuff hiding on the back shelves…things that are already right in front of you at this point in your life can whip up the best batch of Happy you've ever tasted.

The Adventure Pages:

Finding Happiness With What You Have Right Now

How good are you at finding happiness in the moment? If you aren't good, what do you think stops you?

Which "happiness ingredient" is your favorite? Why?

Think of three situations in your life that aren't looking terrific right now. How can you find some happiness in the journey?

Put more arrows in your quiver: What three things do you want to take from this chapter and put to use in your life *right now?*

Here's your Invention Page!

Write down those three arrows on the blank page below. Draw, collage, or otherwise illustrate what your personal "Finding Happiness With What You Have Right Now card" would look like.

Carry Experiences, Not Things

She started walking when she was 45. She walked until she died in 1981, a few days shy of her 73rd birthday. She walked her planned 25,000 miles and so much more, changing thousands upon thousands of lives—while owning nothing but the clothes she wore, and a few small possessions she carried in the pockets of the tunic proclaiming her name and her message. Mildred Norman adopted the name Peace Pilgrim in 1953, the year she first dedicated her life to spreading the word that peace, not war, was the only answer to mankind's woes and chaos.

When she began her pilgrimage, Mildred took a vow to "remain a wanderer until mankind has learned the way of peace, walking until given shelter and fasting until given food." In her 28 years of walking the earth for peace, Mildred spoke to churches, universities, and frequently appeared on local and national radio and television. Peace was Mildred's message, and the lives she touched turned to peace activism as daisies turn toward the sun. Mildred, who owned no material things and was supported by no organization, carried with her every experience she ever had: every questioning voice, every clasped hand, even every argument and mockery.

These intangible things were all she owned, but they were invaluable because every experience enriched her and her message.

This chapter isn't about Peace Pilgrim, however. It's about the idea of carrying experiences, not things.

The premise of the motto, "You can't take it with you," is absolutely true. But we tend to lose sight of this in our day-to-day existence. We forget that we are merely spiritual beings having a human adventure—that inevitably we will transition out of these physical bodies and go on to something else. That's when the idea of stockpiling *stuff* can get in the way of more important experiences that become part of our spiritual road.

I've noticed that people can be divided into four categories: Toys People, Rolodex People, Been-There-Done-That People, and Connection People.

Toys People

The first category contains those who subscribe to the idea that the person who dies with the most toys wins. Toys People amass books, or cars, or Disney objects, or Depression Glass collectibles. They must have the latest gadget, replace their iPhone® device with the newest model, or wait in line overnight during Black Friday sales to get a television that's bigger and better than the one they stood in line for last Christmas. They check out what's trending among their peers. They worry *Does someone else own more? Is their model better than mine?*

Toys People get mad about what they purchased just a few weeks ago because what was good then is no good now—and they're off to find another object to feed their obsession. Somehow, they never get to enjoy what they have because their eyes are always on the next thing.

It's a short walk from amassing to hoarding: being afraid to get rid of anything in case you need it. Material goods can become so overwhelming in a person's life that they crowd out everything else. Eventually, the things own their hoarder rather than the other way around. The hoarder has no room in life for people, experiences, or new possibilities.

Rolodex People

My younger readers may need a definition here, as we have all gone relentlessly digital. The Rolodex used to be the sign of a Big Wheel—the powerful attorney, the Hollywood agent, the corporate mogul. It was a desktop card index used to record names, addresses, and telephone numbers. And its presence proclaimed "this is a person of consequence" to anyone who walked into the Big Wheel's office.

Rolodex People are people collectors. They have dozens of friends and hundreds of acquaintances. They cannot bear to be by themselves, so they are always whirling from one social event to another. They spend inordinate amounts of time on the phone, on the Internet, and on emails and texts to avoid being alone with themselves. They won't make a decision without collective input. At the same time, Rolodex People are not really *there* when they reach out to others because they are too busy looking over their shoulder or at their phone awaiting the next connection in case the current one doesn't fulfill their needs.

Rolodex People believe that other people will be their defense against the dark times of the soul when answers are hard to come by, and the horizon looks fraught with danger. But when no time is spent on cementing relationships to give deep and strong foundations, all those acquaintances disappear like smoke. Rolodex People are left bereft—with absolutely no idea how they lost everyone. They cannot fathom how they will ever work alone.

Been-There-Done-That People

The third category is filled with those for whom experiences are the coin of Life. But, even in this category, there can be toxicity. These are people who rack up concert attendance, who have to visit every single new restaurant that opens, who sit on boards of institutions and museums only to say they are *important* people. These people get virtual hash marks on their experience roster simply because they want more hash marks than anyone else. These people are out to beat others and acquire boasting rights, rather than savor the experience itself.

At the same time, if you ask Been-There-Done-That People how they enjoyed an event or what they got out of the experience, they come up empty. For them, merely being able to say they did something *is* the important part of the experience. The events become much like cotton candy—sweet for a moment, but then melting away with nothing to show for it.

Connection People

The fourth category is for those who both connect with the world and themselves through experiences, and this is where we find the gold of life. If the person volunteers at a kitchen feeding the homeless, there can be the experiences of common goals—compassionately connecting with another human being, and seeing their actions make a concrete difference in the world.

Connecting can be wandering in a city—your hometown or someplace far afield—where you savor the sights, sounds, smells and interactions with the folks who live there. Connecting can include delving into the political process. Connecting can involve volunteering for a cause you believe in. Merely sitting in a park to listen to the birds, watch the squirrels, observe your fellow human beings, and come back to your own solidity as a citizen of the world—that, too, is connecting.

The great part about these experiences is they may not cost you a dime. They take up no space in your house, on your contacts list, or anywhere else with limited space or resources. These encounters and meeting points can be carried forward with no more effort than a thought, an emotion, a remembrance. But the small space they take up is eclipsed so much by what they give back.

The You Can't Take It With You Experiment

Let's try an experiment:

Imagine yourself at a very old age (you choose the number). You know that there are many, many more days behind you than ahead of you, and you don't have much more time.

You are sitting in your living room at dusk, looking around at all the *stuff* you have collected throughout your lifetime. This *stuff* tells you who you were, and what you did with your life as a whole. When you step into the Afterlife, you will have no more effect on this *stuff*, and it will no longer affect you.

Look at your collection of things. Do not focus on family memories or attachments—just you and this world of things. Some are beautiful, yes. With some, you can't even remember why you desired them. When you die, these items will all go to other people, with no trace of you or why you bought them. Were they worth the space they took up in your life?

Now look at all the people you have collected (if you're a Rolodex Person*).* Flip through the mental picture book. How many of them think of you the way you think of them? In fact, do you think of some or any of them at all? How many can you actually remember? How many people played an important part in your life? Or are they all merely names on a roster?

Look at your list of events. How many of them made a difference in your life? How many helped you grow, change, or bloom? How many would you do over again if you could? How many trigger no lasting memories at all?

Look at the true experiences in your life, times when you were there on all levels: physically, mentally, emotionally, spiritually. How have they changed you? How have your actions and spirit changed the lives you've touched by being part of those moments? How much *good* are you leaving behind you for having experienced those things?

No matter who we are—famous or anonymous, rich or poor, genius or Average Bob—we are asked by Spirit to leave the world a little better than we found it. It's part of our spiritual DNA. When we truly *live* our experiences—giving and taking within them—and allowing those experiences to mold our minds and hearts, we pile up untold riches that we can, indeed, take with us when we go.

Rather than fading into the mists of time, those experiences may plant the seeds for others to grow, change, live and thrive long after we are gone.

The Adventure Pages:

Carrying Experiences, Not Things

Of the four kinds of people in this chapter, which are you?

What does being that kind of person bring to your life?

Which of the four kinds of people do you like to have in your life? Why?

What three experiences in your life have resonated through the years? What did they bring you that you still have and cherish?

What did you learn through that "sunset of your life" visualization?

Put more arrows in your quiver: What three things do you want to take from this chapter and put to use in your life right now?

Here's your Invention Page!

Write down those three arrows on the blank page below. Draw, collage, or otherwise illustrate what your personal "Carry Experiences, Not Things card" would look like.

What To Do With Stuff When You've Lightened Your Load

As we leave our wants, guilts, and avidity behind, we give ourselves more space to simply live. We give ourselves a better chance to savor what we have, rather than watch things pile up. We find that we can relax when we're not always chasing after something we don't have. But when we are downsizing…well, Stuff doesn't just go *poof* and disappear. We need to find new homes for what's useful. We need to decide where and how to dump Stuff that's no longer something we want to carry with us so we can ensure our life is cleared out rather than simply moving piles from one spot to another.

So, what *do* you do with all the things you've decided you no longer need? Well, it depends if the items in question are physical, mental, emotional or spiritual. Each category has specific ways you can send things off to another part of the Universe.

Physical Items

The reason the old saying "One man's trash is another man's treasure" has been around for so long is that it's true. If you have spent time going through your house and life, you will have a pile of Stuff that no longer serves any purpose. Could be that you've outgrown them, they're broken, or they were never sufficiently *you* in the first place. Whatever the reason they are in the "goodbye" pile, there are four things you can do.

Mend them. If you have an item that is broken but you would still use if it were fixed, see if it can be patched up. That pod coffee maker? See if cleaning it out with vinegar or other clarifying agents (my husband calls it "pickling") can get it working again. Those favorite sheets that have a few pokes and tears where the cats have climbed up for bedtime snuggles? Get out a needle, thread, and darn them. If you can repair something instead of replacing it, do so. In our throw-away and planned-obsolescence society, we're not used to refurbishing things when they cease to function perfectly. Give it a try, and get ready to be shocked at how much you save.

Give them away. If there is something you no longer use, but someone else would want, donate it so others can enjoy it. If your clothing is still in decent shape, find a consignment store. Gift your goods to Goodwill, the Salvation Army, or another organization that resells gently used items. Some of these places also take toys, small appliances, books, and other useful household goods. If you're the kind of person who enjoys meeting strangers, hold a garage sale! A garage sale requires more work than just sending your no-longer-needed surplus to someone else, but it might make you a few dollars. Watching someone pick up one of your items and exclaiming, "I've been looking for an old-fashioned lemon squeezer for two years!" while grinning from ear to ear, is delicious.

Transform them. This step is where your creative artistry comes in. Have something that didn't work for one purpose but might work for another? With a little thought and imagination, give it a go and see what you can invent from the things you already have. We had a pile of old cork squares from a soundproofing project that went nowhere. Then, one day, I needed a larger-than-life bulletin board for my office that would literally cover half of the wall. Rather than spending hundreds of dollars for such a thing at the office supply store, Carle measured twice, cut once, stuck the cork tiles on the wall, and framed them with a bit of edging—giving me the board of my dreams for less than ten dollars.

Dump them. Some things are no longer of any use to anyone: non-rechargeable batteries, catnip toys that have been played out and shredded, kids' toys that are beyond redemption, cracked plates, out-of-date medicines. Get rid of these things without a second thought. Be sure to dispose of them appropriately (hazardous waste days, returned drug drop-off days in your community, recycle stations, and so on).

For the mental items, however, the dumping process is not quite as cut-and-dry as it is for physical things.

Mental Items

When old ideas or old self-talk are what's going in the rubbish tip, there are three things to do with them.

Extract the lessons. Before you dump them, look carefully at certain thoughts you had and what they brought to your life. Observe where a belief of not-good-enough made it so. Watch where other people bought your negative self-judgments, and what happened when you stopped thinking that way. Make sure you understand why such self-talk was actually self-defeating. But do it with compassion for who you were then and who you are now. Don't make it a last opportunity to beat yourself up for not being perfect.

Draw a line under them. Acknowledge the old memes and then plant the intention, very strongly, that you are done with these things. No need to reuse what isn't useful. Remind yourself that you don't want to think these things anymore. Using them to threaten, frighten, or guilt yourself into making changes actually gives them power. If they no longer have power, then you don't need to recall them.

Find replacements that work. While we can empty physical closets and enjoy the newfound empty space, the mind is not so easily tamed. Your mind will spend its time thinking, observing, judging and questioning. There are several books out there about reprogramming how we think about ourselves; my favorite is Michael Losier's *Law of Attraction: The Science of Attracting More of What You Want and Less of What You Don't*.

Emotional Items

These are the old fears, anxieties, dreads, guilts, angers—the emotional toxic dump that we revisit time and again because it seems to be all we know. Try these three ways to loosen their grip:

Thank them before you throw them out. As with the mental trash, these emotions were felt because we believed they would keep us safe, make us happy, be the right answer to certain situations—at the time. And while there is a very good chance they did help in some way that you understood then, they are no longer needed now.

Use the lessons to help others. We can use stories of old emotions, and our reactions to them, to teach others. These lessons freeze-dry in our minds. They can be reconstituted to teach others as needed, but they don't take up a lot of room in our own emotional pantry. We can show others what we did. We can teach others how we decided an experience or decision did not work for us. We can share how we made shifts to reassure others that they, too, can change their emotional landscape. If someone comes at you with a repeat of an old toxic situation you're done with, you'll be able to respond rather than impulsively react because you'll understand the origin of your own emotions.

Draw strength from them. Make a point of seeing how certain emotional responses that are no longer who you are have propelled you onto the road you need to walk now. Recall a time you needed to show bravado you did not have; when you were angry, but the resulting fallout softened you and healed a situation. Draw strength from the idea that you did the best you could within each situation. Recognize that you have taken the lessons and incorporated them. Doing so will give you the tools to respond accordingly the next time a similar circumstance comes up.

Spiritual Items

Even spiritual situations can be left behind if they are no longer serving us. What can you do?

Have compassion. Understand that when we are in a spiritual "dark night of the soul," it is because our soul, Spirit and pre-birth plan are asking us to move to a different place in our incarnational pattern. What we believed once does not have to be what we believe always.

Bless and release If there are spiritual roads we once traveled, that no longer take us where we want to go, bless them for the lessons and release them gently. If there are spiritual groups we once belonged to—that have become toxic for one reason or another—bless and release them as well. All things change, and spirituality can and does count as changeable.

Change without condemning. The spiritual road, more than any other place in our lives, is the one where logic rarely resides. If you held a particular religious ideation and moved on to something else—or even nothing else—avoid condemning those who still believe. Marcy converted from Jewish to Baptist. Denise converted from Catholic to Wiccan. John converted from Neopaganism to Jewish. Kevin had tried several different spiritual roads before he decided none of them worked for him; he now counts himself as agnostic. No one has a right to tell anyone else that what they believe is "wrong." Spirituality is always, first and foremost, one's personal connection to God, Spirit, or All That Is. The key word here is personal. Feel free to change, review and reorient your spiritual center without the need to grab others' compasses and shake them, too.

Now that we are at the end of our exploration of *Living Well With Less*, walk through your Life house the way we did at the beginning of Part II. Notice how your Life house has changed and shifted. How do you feel? Do you have more breathing space? Do you know better, now, what you truly own? If so, your clean-out project is a sparkling success.

The Adventure Pages:

What To Do With Stuff When You've Lightened Your Load

Where do you need to lighten your load the most (physically, mentally, emotionally, spiritually)?

Where will it be easiest to lighten your load? Why?

Do you panic or feel relieved at the thought of getting rid of a lot of Stuff? Why?

Imagine your life streamlined: everything cleaned out, and your life filled with only that which supports you. What would you do with that extra space and time you create?

Put more arrows in your quiver: What three things do you want to take from this chapter and put to use in your life *right now*?

Here's your Invention Page!

Write down those three arrows on the blank page below. Draw, collage, or otherwise illustrate what your personal "What To Do With Stuff card" would look like.

Part III: Going With the Flow, Learning To Adapt

Why Perfect Isn't What You Think It Is

We think of perfect, and so many things come to mind: the flawless movie star, the cake without a crumb or a fleck of icing out of place, the straight A report card, the pristine lake view. Perfection, to most people, means nothing to improve upon—that nothing is wrong nor needs to change. *Perfect* is as good as it can possibly get.

Good grief! I don't know about you, but *perfect* sounds boring to me if that's the definition!

Let's take a look at a non-perfect day to see what perfection can *really* be.

This year, my 61st birthday was not as celebratory as last year's by any means. Medical circumstances had me on heavy antibiotics, which caused a lot of side effects and required a restricted diet. My husband had to work late, so I spent my birthday alone rather than venturing out to a spectacular restaurant with him as we usually would do (plus, see "medical"). When I started writing this chapter originally, it was for a blog post that had already been due the week before—and I had another post due that same week—so my deadlines were blinking red. I *never* work on my birthday, typically, but I had to this time to keep on schedule. My husband and I had both been insanely busy; there was nary a card or present in sight.

Believe it or not, I looked at the day and thought, *You know what? It's really perfect.*

Why? Because I chose to see what was behind the circumstances Life handed me. I decided I would happily explore what *could* be done and what unexpected gifts might result from these unplanned, un-perfect-appearing states of affairs.

Let's see what was perfect about this situation.

Perfection Ponder #1:

Perfection can be flexible. To be honest, with the amount of work I had to do and feeling the weight of my writing deadlines, I needed to take every *good* day I had on this medical regimen and make it count. I'd done this particular dance before. I knew there would definitely be downtime days when antibiotics would make me too tired or too ill to concentrate. *Those* were the days that would demand that I do nothing more than to curl up with a cat, my cup of tea, and a do-nothing mind. My 61st birthday, luckily, wasn't want of them.

Perfection Ponder #2:

Perfection can mean considering other ideas and changing course. When I started writing this chapter, I delighted in seeing what other people had to say on the subject because it might spark me to take a different or additional direction. If I felt as though a particular point belonged in the text but might be slanted a different way, I would contact a friend to get feedback. That little back-and-forth always gave me a feeling of warmth and connection.

Perfection Ponder #3:

Perfection can give attention to what really matters. Knowing that I was doing something I love—rather than regimenting it into only certain days and times—meant that when the Muse called, I was free to pursue its tantalizing music. I didn't need to check my appointment book to see if I was available. Inspiration can hit like a lightning flash, and will often ask you to drop whatever you are doing to catch that lightning.

Perfection Ponder #4:

Perfection can be found in the tiniest moments and the most ordinary occurrences. Being at my desk that day, instead of running around celebrating my birthday, allowed me to have quiet moments to appreciate all that I do have: a sharp mind, a facility with words, a reliable computer, a view outside my window to our hayfield and hills, and a pair of beloved Maine Coons snoozing on their cat tree sending out their "Everything's fine, Mom!" vibes with every schnurr.

Perfection Ponder #5:

Perfection can be the willingness to "fail fast" and get it out of the way to get where you want to go. Writing with a deadline means I need to get ideas down fast; I don't necessarily have the luxury of pondering. I wrote several pages the morning of my birthday, some of which I ultimately tossed when I realized they were not getting me where I wanted to go. Because I was not writing as slowly and thoughtfully as I usually would, I quickly saw what was and not working. And I had no compunction about tossing out whole paragraphs to get to the meat of the matter more succinctly.

Perfection Ponder #6:

Perfection can be flow rather than fraught. Because I had been willing to be easy about the day and refused to compare it unfavorably to other birthdays, I was able to take everything in stride. My blood pressure stayed steady. My heart and mind were at ease. As a result, my immune system was busy boosting itself and helping me heal.

Perfection Ponder #7:

Much perfection comes from imperfection. Ten or twenty years ago I would have had a veritable "conniption fit" when plans were upended as thoroughly as they were this birthday. In the decades since, I had to learn how to respond—rather than react—and accept that the Universe usually has things well in hand. I learned to recognize what could be done to improve a situation rather than fight it or get angry. Because I had allowed myself—this time around—to trust that everything I was going to discover in the upended plans would be fun and beneficial, it happened. As it usually does!

Perfection Ponder #8:

The Universe is always perfect. We are part of the Universe. The Universe is always perfect. Therefore, our situation is always perfect—whether or not it looks that way on the surface. The Universe's greatest gift to me on my 61st birthday was supporting me in perfectly Living the Examined Life.

I was able to look at the whole situation and, while acknowledging it wasn't cloaking itself in a traditional happy birthday vibe, I recognized that it did have its own useful structure. I was able to move forward with my understanding of Life and thus my ability to take any given situation and drink up every possible good and happy thing I could find.

That's a whole lot of finding perfection in perceived imperfection, isn't it?

What I want for you to see here is that the idea of perfection as something rigid, rarely attainable, and *the only good thing* is far from what I call "Useful Truth." Life can look so beautifully different when we accept that that perfection is relative—not rigid. Perfection can be found in any situation if we alter our squint on the world and look behind the curtain. Then, every single day can have a bounty of perfection in it for us to take in, enjoy, and use.

The Adventure Pages:

Why Perfect Isn't What You Think It Is

Has Perfect been a friend or foe in your life? Why?

When did the search for perfection stop you from doing something important? How so?

\Think of a challenging situation and find three perfect things about it. How do your feelings about the situation change?

Put more arrows in your quiver: What three things do you want to take from this chapter and put to use in your life right now?

Here's your Invention Page!

Write down those three arrows on the blank page below. Draw, collage, or otherwise illustrate what your personal "Why Perfection Isn't What You Think It Is card" would look like.

Stumbling Toward Enlightenment

I love the phrase "stumbling toward enlightenment." I came across it initially when I found Parang Geri Larkin's book, which uses this phrase as the title. Larkin was a high-level corporate executive who started meditating because she had a twitch in one eye that wouldn't stop. Fast forward to today, Larkin is a beloved Dharma teacher and founder of the Still Point Zen Buddhist Temple in Detroit—long gone from the corporate world. Larkin is still a student, still learning. For her, there is no perfection. There is no "I have done *this* and *this* and *this*; therefore, everything is fine as it is." There is always looking at life, looking at one's reaction to it, and asking yet another Koan.

What is a Koan? In Zen Buddhism, a Koan is an unanswerable question to show one the inadequacy of logical reasoning and to provoke enlightenment.

Much of life is made up of Koans.

Larkin's writing captured me because of how authentic she is. She writes about her own backtracking and trip-ups as she sought to find peace and centeredness around her world and life path. Larkin's writing style resonates with me: taking earnest, deep subjects and bringing them down from the mountain. She is real and honest, sharing her difficulties and joys along her own trek. Chapters in the book like "The Invaluable Lesson of Miserable Days," "When All You Still Think About Is Sex," and "Relax, My Darling" bring her home truths and philosophy to an accessible place. Her writing allows me to see a bit of myself in her, and makes me think, *Wow! Maybe I can do that, too.*

When looking at the philosophy of perfection, it's important to understand the value of stumbling. Think for a moment about the action of stumbling. First, you become acutely aware that your footing is faulty. Then, everything slips into high focus. You notice your foot, the pitch forward or backward, and how your muscles tense to break what might be a fall. After you get yourself rebalanced, you look at your surroundings to identify what caused the stumble. Finally, you make a mental note to watch out for the culprit next time.

Imagine if you had just strolled on by instead of examining what caused the imbalance. Ignoring the culprit can dull your awareness and make the next misstep possibly worse. The next time around, you might take a deep plunge and end up shattering something precious (a fragile object you were holding in your hands or even your own limbs). But since you only tripped a little, you've become tuned into your surroundings and can avoid it next time. The stumble, instead of being a slip-up, becomes a gift.

Life can be like that stumble. There's an advantage to learning by acknowledging the mistakes, double-backs, and bad judgment calls as simple miscalculations that teach you how to prevent pitfalls in the future. And we're not only talking about those particular situations where the lessons can be useful. Missteps in our surroundings remind us to watch our step in other situations as well—even ones that are constructed very differently.

When we do something that is not good for us, we can miss an opportunity. Let's say we react instead of respond to an emotional situation. Piling fault upon fault is the last thing we need to do. To berate ourselves for the mistake and beat ourselves up for getting it wrong entirely contradicts the opportunity to learn. We may laugh at the meme "The beatings will continue until morale improves." But we have to ask ourselves, *Is this the way I deal with my own blunders?*

When a child stumbles, the mother does not tell him he's stupid as he lies there crying. She doesn't say, "I'm going to make you stumble again until you get it right." She picks up the child and comforts him. Then, she shows him where the crack in the pavement exists so the child can avoid stumbling over it in the future. The mother is nurturing. She uses the stumble as a tender teaching moment and reassures the child that he is worthy of love no matter what.

The Universe is always willing to work with us when our actions take us away from where we want to be, away from Enlightenment. The key is to turn the idea of stumbling on its ear. It is very easy to count all of our mistakes, our screw-ups, and our failings. But if we are very observant, we can also see how stumbling taught us and presented a more useful perspective.

Six Degrees Of Successful Stumbling

Remember playing "Six Degrees of Kevin Bacon?" In this game, you can think of any actor and, within six moves, find out that they connect to Kevin Bacon through acting, marriage, charities, or what have you.

You can do the same sort of thing with a point of stumbling and a point of enlightenment. Let's look at some examples and make those connections together.

Getting fired from my job led me to marry the man of my dreams:

Because I kept getting fired from jobs, I decided I would work for myself.

Because I worked for myself, I discovered I did not need to rely on a man for financial well-being.

Because I didn't need to rely on a man for financial well-being, I didn't feel desperate to marry.

Because I didn't feel desperate to marry, I chose to have relationships with men I could trust, rather than men with money.

Because I changed the parameters around what kind of a man was good for me, I met my Carle.

Because I met Carle, I discovered that what I was truly seeking wasn't money or simple security, but a trustworthy, funny, honest, and best friend.

And so I married the man of my dreams.

Was it a completely smooth road? Of course not; I'm very human. Working for myself has had its ups and downs (and still does). I kissed a lot of frogs, even with the different parameters, before I met my prince. And it took a few years to mutually knock the rough edges and bachelor-think off both of us since we each had been on our own for over a decade apiece before starting a relationship.

Janet's abuse led her to help the abused:

Janet came from a very abusive family. She fought constantly and got into trouble from dawn to dusk—never knowing when her mother would hit her or her father would "gaslight" her (taking her to task for something she knew she hadn't done). She decided she no longer wanted to carry the weight of the abuse and crazy behavior inflicted on her growing up.

Because she chose not to continue carrying this burden, she became the family rebel.

Because she became the family rebel, she learned to question others' limitations on her.

Because she chose to question limitations, she explored her own boundaries actively.

Because she explored her boundaries, she found methods of self-work that changed her life.

Because she found self-work that changed her life, she learned how to find her own answers.

Because she learned to find her own answers, she became a master teacher with a bestselling book helping others to do the same thing.

My challenge to you is to embrace your stumblings. Find all the things you think are problematic, the places where you cringe when you think about them. Instead of using them to beat yourself up, view them with love, compassion, and the curiosity of a Martian detective. You will discover how these stumblings have given you enlightenment, clarity, and incredible new roads to follow.

The Adventure Pages:

Stumbling Toward Enlightenment

Think of a time you've stumbled. What did you learn from the event that you later used?

Do the Six Degrees of Perfect Stumbling exercise with that event. What did you gain unexpectedly as a result of what happened?

Think of a friend who is always, in his/her mind, making mistakes. How might you present this idea to them? How would you work with it?

Put more arrows in your quiver: What three things do you want to take from this chapter and put to use in your life right now?

Here's your Invention Page!

Write down those three arrows on the blank page below. Draw, collage, or otherwise illustrate what your personal "Stumbling Toward Enlightenment card" would look like.

How Perfect Destroys Good

When we are striving hard to make everything just so, we lose the joy of *doing*. We become angrier and angrier at ourselves for not getting it right. We pile mistake onto mistake and berate ourselves unmercifully. At that point, the simple thing we wanted to do or the goal we set for ourselves becomes toxic, anathema, and we chalk it up as one more failure because we cannot bear to continue.

What we're talking about here is something as simple as a recipe or as all-encompassing as choosing a partner or career. I want to show you how life-changing it can be to accept good over perfect, by sharing with you the example of my parents, Jerry and Frances, and my stepmother, Shirley.

My mother, Frances, was first generation Jewish-American. She was the daughter of Russian-German immigrants, and the baby of three children. Her older brothers were bigger both in stature (they were well over six feet while she was five-two) and age (nine and ten years older), and they doted on her. While she grew up poor in Tidewater Virginia, she was motivated enough to go to Sinai Hospital Nursing School, earn her cap, and become a superb registered nurse.

She met Jerry, a bright but quiet boy from New Jersey, when she was a nursing student. He was an intern at Johns Hopkins. They fell in love and decided to get married.

However, when Jerry introduced Frances to his parents, David and Margaret, Frances was irreparably damaged by his mother's initial reaction. Horrified that her personal plans for her son had gone so terribly awry, Margaret made it clear that Frances was everything she did not want in a daughter-in-law. She actually screamed at her son, "How could you *do* this to us!" And then promptly fainted at that first, awful meeting.

Margaret wanted the perfect match for her boy. In her mind, Jerry should have married a girl who was smarter, prettier, classier, and certainly wealthier than this plain Southern girl who was raised above a corner store. There was no room in her heart and mind for *good enough*. Margaret's perfect dreams for her boy were ruined. And for the next forty years, no matter what Frances did, said, or tried, Margaret was her blatant, supercilious enemy. Whether it was striving to be a good wife, raising my brother and me, or keeping house, Margaret relentlessly told Frances how inadequate she was at every task.

For my mother, the clothing, jewelry, furs, and magnificent house that my father bought her were how she came to measure herself against others—and against her fears. She never left the house less than perfectly dressed and coiffed, her makeup flawless even if all she was doing was going to the grocery store. My mother worked hard at "being cultured." Still, she always felt inadequate as though she was missing something that would make her *good enough* in other people's eyes—and, therefore, her own. She never felt competent enough to deal with my father's brilliance, nor did she understand it. And when it was clear that her children had inherited his high IQ and creativity, she felt isolated in inadequacy.

My mother was never expected to be perfect growing up. She was good, and her family was proud of her. She didn't go to college; she went to nursing school. She didn't start a business the way her brothers did, but she was good at her job. She was "Faygie," (Yiddish for "little bird") and she was loved for who she was.

My father's story was the exact opposite. The family legend has it that, while pregnant with my father, my grandmother would sit and test out which first and middle names sounded grandest with "Dorkin, M.D." after them. She had my father's life planned out: He'd finish high school with honors, attend his father's alma mater, go to the best medical school, and then return home to practice medicine in Camden after graduation. She had an iron dragon grip on everyone in the family: her husband, her younger son Arnold, and my father. Everything was perfect if you did it Margaret's way. And if you didn't, there was no reasoning with Margaret—you failed. This all-or-nothing family trope guaranteed that my father would be caught in the Perfection Trap all his life. As a result, he was unable to come to his wife's defense when his mother constantly crushed Frances' spirit. He already knew the cost of defying his mother.

For years I wondered what it would feel like just to be accepted without judgment. To have a family that loved you no matter what, and didn't make you pay for your failings in emotional coin. I believed I would never experience such a healing existence.

And, then, along came Shirley.

The spring of 1984 brought two deaths. My grandmother finally succumbed to congestive heart failure in February at age 86. Tragically, my mother followed her only one month later, dying of a heart attack at age 59. For the first time in his life, my father was completely adrift, with no one shouting at him about not being enough. Then, a few months later, family friends introduced Dad to Shirley Wells.

Shirley was as different from my mother as one could be. Shirley could trace her ancestors back to 1620 Sweden. She grew up in Revolutionary War-tinged Haddonfield, New Jersey. She owned a horse as a child and rode as naturally as some people walk. Her first marriage had been to an architect with whom she traveled the world, and who gave her three marvelous children: Kappy, John, and Sam.

She was absolutely unself-conscious, a beautiful woman with bright aqua eyes. She'd wear a bit of lipstick and mascara, nothing else. She wore no jewelry on a regular basis except for her wedding ring and my father's Phi Beta Kappa key on a chain around her neck. An insightful and inventive landscape designer by trade, Shirley would cheerfully cut our lawn in jeans and bare feet—my father always worrying she'd cut off a toe. She loved music and poetry and delighted in my father's intellectual prowess—and he blossomed under her beaming gaze. He wrote her poetry (some of which was later published), sent her a constant stream of flowers, burned up the telephone lines the year that they courted, and married her triumphantly a year after my mother died.

Shirley had never been told that perfection was her only goal, and would tell the world what she was worth. She knew that perfection was sometimes not attainable, and she knew how to love what she had. When her first husband left her, Shirley did not fall apart; she moved on. She got her landscaping credentials in her fifties. When she married Dad, she worked hard at blending the two families. And as stepmothers go, Shirley was one of the wonderful ones. She loved me, my husband, my brother's family and his children as if we were her own. She made it her business to give Carle and me a glorious wedding at the house the year after Dad died. And out of everyone in the family, Shirley was the one who truly *got* what I did, and delighted in it. She said over and over how much of my father she saw in me, and how happy it made her. She was, first to last, a compassionate and loving human being.

Comparing Shirley and Frances is not to say that one was good and the other was not. In the beginning, both women were loved and cherished by their families. It is a clear example that perfection chasing can crush a spirit beyond repair. If my grandmother had accepted my mother, Mom and Dad might have been able to create a true partnership—not a thirty-eight-year battle of sadness and disappointment. Because my grandmother was not in the picture when Dad remarried, Shirley was able to make a very different marriage with him: where flaws, imperfections, and eccentricities were not things to complain about, but rather personality traits to work with, accept and even celebrate.

I encourage you to look at all the relationships you have with your family, your friends, your work, and your goals. Compassionately but unflinchingly examine all the places where perfect overcame good; where your insistence on all-or-nothing took joy, possibility and love, and turned it inside out.

Remember that every moment of possibility resides in Now. If you see places where you need to make course corrections, do it. And do so without worrying whether that takes away from perfect. Because perfection—true perfection—is in the moment. This moment is perfect. And that's all the good you need to have at your side.

The Adventure Pages:

How Perfect Destroys Good

Where do you "beat yourself up" most often? Why?

Reimagine one of those times with the idea that Good can triumph over Perfect. What does it look like now?

How would your life change if you stopped thinking perfection was the only correct response to a project or situation?

Put more arrows in your quiver: What three things do you want to take from this chapter and put to use in your life right now?

Here's your Invention Page!

Write down those three arrows on the blank page below. Draw, collage, or otherwise illustrate what your personal "How Perfect Destroys Good card" would look like.

When To Stand Your Ground

In Part III, we have been talking about adaptability, going with the flow, and misconceptions about what perfection and imperfection actually are. But as the saying goes, "Sometimes exceptions prove the rule."

There are times when standing your ground is the right (sometimes *only*) idea. No, we are not talking about the "Stand Your Ground" law around shootings and gun violence. We're talking about the way we feel pushed around on an everyday basis. Whether it's by someone who will not take "No" for an answer, or someone asking us to go against our own principles in an extreme way, or someone trying to guilt and scare us into thinking the way they do, standing your ground may be the only answer.

It's true even when you find yourself staring at your reflection in the mirror, with doubt gazing back at you in that unshielded regard. Sometimes standing your ground is the only answer that gets you where you want to go. When we are fighting addictions of any kind (food, tobacco, drugs, alcohol, or some emotional toxicity) slippage, while it may happen, is nothing to be condoned or accepted as "just the way of things." We must hold ourselves to what is true, what is right for us, what is our center.

Sometimes this can be extremely difficult when we are moving away from situations or people. My client, Celia, was mentored for decades by a woman who was strong, brilliant in her field, and absolutely knew *who* she was. The mentor had a particular way of looking at and acting in the world, and my client tried to emulate her for years. It was a difficult road. Often in striving to be like her mentor, Celia would "go off the rails" in terms of who she thought herself to be. Celia would directly contradict her own heart and mind, insisting to herself she was wrong because it wasn't the way her mentor would handle things. The mentor—believing staunchly in her own worldview—only made things worse, not better, by agreeing that what Celia was feeling and thinking was the wrong way to go. By measuring herself in large and small ways against a woman whose circumstances were light-years away from her own, Celia was mired in constant self-doubt. Just walking into this woman's presence, Celia felt her own lack.

Eventually, Celia became an entrepreneur in her own right in an entirely different field. She gained confidence in who she was and how she saw the world around her. She began to know her own truths. Still, whenever she and her mentor got together, there would be the subtle (or not so subtle) hints that however Celia saw the world and her own place in it, she was wrong. That she was responding inappropriately. That she simply wasn't as good as her former mentor at navigating her own soul and life path—and never would be.

Celia doesn't speak with her mentor much anymore. "It was a wrench," she admits. "I thought we'd be friends forever. But eventually, I realized that she wasn't always right and that the strongest and the best thing I could do for myself was to bless her and release her to live her own life, as I live mine. If I was going to be who I was meant to be, I had to stand my ground, even if that meant losing her friendship."

That situation and Celia's decision regarding the friendship are together a perfect example of my favorite Thomas Jefferson quote: "In style, swim with the current; in principle, stand like a rock."

When I've spoken about adaptability, going with the flow, and allowing change to be perfect, I refer to the details in a project—the ebb and flow of a relationship, the constant striving to be the best person we can.

Even when it comes to your belief systems, I encourage you to listen to other points of view. See if you want to change your understanding as a result. You might even find your current beliefs fitting you better if you adjust your perspective. For example, if you believe that your health is the most important thing in your life, you may stand strongly on the side of exercise, supplements, and a certain way of eating. Yet others may bring your attention to their ways of taking care of their health, which excludes some of the things you believe to be vital or includes things you never thought about before. As a result, you may decide to ditch a supplement regimen and eat more unprocessed and whole foods. You may recognize that stress and lack of sleep are playing a detrimental part in your health regimen.

Thus, you make changes. That's adaptability.

On the other hand, if your friend believes staunchly that we should "eat, drink and be merry, for tomorrow we die" and they drink and smoke, their ways of self-care are directly opposed to what you know and believe. So, stand your ground. If being around tobacco smoke is a detriment to you, do not let them smoke in your house, especially if that is your house rule.

Here's one of those everyday examples:

Renata and her husband, Garth, have some definite house rules around food. Because diabetes is rampant in both families, she runs her household on the low-carb and whole foods principle. Her children (four-year-old Ella and seven-year-old Marta) are healthy and have grown up with the idea that desserts are rare treats. You eat enough at lunch to take you through to dinner, and junk food is just that—junk.

Most of the time, Renata has no problem enforcing the house rules. But when her mother-in-law, Madge, comes over, all of those rules go out the window. As Madge sits down during a visit with the kids, she chuckles while opening her purse to pull out a package of Twizzlers® licorice and some Mega-Stuff Oreo® cookies. "Oh, your mother is being silly," she croons. "All kids need treats sometimes." Marta knows to say "No." But often, Ella is still tempted. She eats too much sugar, gets ill and bad-tempered, and there is always a scene. Madge gets huffy and accuses Renata of being a tyrant of a parent until Garth steps in and puts his foot down. And it happens every single time Madge visits.

To put a stop to this, Garth puts a new house rule in place: Madge is not allowed to bring *any* food to the house. *Ever.* And if she is found feeding the kids contraband, she is out the door.

Informing her of the new arrangement, Garth has to face the Wrath of Madge. After all, being The Mother-In-Law and The Grandmother, she has rights!

Well, no, she doesn't. Not if those rights compromise the health of Ella and Marta.

Fast forward about eight months. Madge has accepted that "No" means no, even to her. She wants to see her grandchildren more than she wants to be right. So now, what comes out of the purse are Mad Libs books and puzzles, which suits everyone just fine.

I've given you examples with mentors and with family. But standing your ground is important in the Wide World itself. To address today's worldview, you may believe that the way to peace is reaching out through interfaith alliances or changing the current economic strata. If that's the case, then don't let the naysayers (who are calling you a fool and threatening you with their way of life) make you back down. Yes, we will need to compromise. We will need to come into balance and cooperation with each other. But compromise means each party is giving in a little bit to reach a useful mid-ground. You don't need to go from one side of your belief systems all the way to the other out of fear or under duress. That's not compromise or adaptability; that's caving in.

As we close out the chapter on adaptability, I encourage you to look at your life as a whole. What's perfect for you? What are you willing to change? What is the core of your soul that you wouldn't trade for diamonds and power? When you know how your life is structured, what you will compromise on and what must stay solid in its own essence?

Enjoy discovering and owning the way *you* want to live your life, and how you want to move in the world—at least for now. When you do, you will find that adaptability is as easy as putting one foot in front of the other.

The Adventure Pages:

When To Stand Your Ground

Think of a time when you knew you had to stand your ground—on a belief, in a relationship, on self-care. How did you do it?

There are times for compromise and adaptability, and times to stand your ground. How do you differentiate these for yourself?

What is a good "rule of thumb" for you when you need to stand your ground yet remain comfortable in a situation? What behavior will support you?

Put more arrows in your quiver: What three things do you want to take from this chapter and put to use in your life right now?

Here's your Invention Page!

Write down those three arrows on the blank page below. Draw, collage, or otherwise illustrate what your personal "When To Stand Your Ground card" would look like.

Part IV: Stress Is a Complicated Friend

Is Stress Good Or Bad?

These days, people hear the word *stress* and think of someone tearing their hair out, screaming at the kids, taking headache pills, or dropping dead of a heart attack. Stress can often be seen as something horrific—something to avoid at all costs—while, at the same time, it's an inevitable part of modern life. With some people, if they aren't under stress, they think something is wrong. They equate the word stress with productivity, success, and accomplishment. Well, they're right, and they're wrong.

People are mistakenly lumping stress into one pile when it's actually at least two. *Eustress* is what we would consider "good stress." Good stress is the energy that gets triggered when you have a challenge to meet—that motivator helping you to reach a goal. It can help you get out of a bad situation when hair-trigger reflexes are necessary (that's the old fight-or-flight mechanism coming into play). It can help you organize faster, concentrate more sharply, and hit that goal line. But stress is only good when you use it in positive, self-building ways—such as pumping you up when you compete in a sports event or giving you that extra *sparkle* in an audition.

The occasional ping of good stress can strengthen your immune system, keep your brain cells at their ultimate performance level, improve heart function, and make surgery recovery go faster and smoother. Good stress can make you more alert, better equipped to make decisions, and gets your heart, muscles, and blood flow running at peak performance so you can compete at your best.

"Wait a minute," you're saying. "All that stuff about heart rate and muscles and blood flow—isn't that the *bad* stuff?"

Eustress turns into distress when it's chronic. Here are some examples:

☐ When deadlines feel like you will never meet them, and you are always saying "Yes" when you should be saying "No" (piling the mountain of tasks on top of an already overburdened schedule), that's chronic stress.

☐ When you second-guess yourself and others all the time, trying to figure out every angle of a situation out of underlying fear or anger, that's chronic stress.

☐ When you never feel you are good enough, and you become the constantly carping voice inside your own head, that's chronic stress.

☐ When you obsess over situations that have yet to occur or are just theoretical, that's chronic stress.

☐ When you are persistently anxious or depressed, that's chronic stress.

Chronic stress is one of the most harmful things to which you can subject yourself. Chronic stress opens the door to addictions, adrenal fatigue, back pain, cancer, chronic digestive difficulties, a depressed immune system, depression, fatigue, harmful behaviors, headaches, heart disease, high blood pressure, strokes...do we really need to go on?

There are subsets of bad stress as well: hyperstress (too much) and hypostress (too little).

Hyperstress

Hyperstress is the stress version of "the straw that broke the camel's back." You're likely to have hyperstress if you work for one of those bosses who believes that taking lunch means you're slacking, and work should be 24/7. Such bigwigs don't believe in priority lists unless everything is an "A" priority.

Another place that hyperstress lives is in one-person entrepreneurial businesses: everything needs to get done, there is no one else to do it, and you can't afford to hire an assistant, so you work like three people but give yourself no breathing space for even one.

When we are subjected to hyperstress for too long, we break. It might look like an emotional breakdown. It might mean we show up to work one day with a gun. It might mean we strip off our clothes in the lunchroom and rant at the top of our lungs. It might even mean suicide looks like the only viable alternative. These may sound like extreme examples, but under extreme stress, we can reach a breaking point where we are willing to do anything to stop the pain. Even a coyote will chew off its own foot to get out of a trap; this is the human version of that desperate decision.

Hypostress

Hypostress goes the other direction. We've all had days when we can't find anything to settle on; nothing interests us, boredom seems overwhelming, and we simply can't be motivated. We bounce from thing to thing. We wander around the house. We look aimlessly into the refrigerator twelve times. In this version of stress, you simply do not have enough challenging you in one of the good ways.

What are some of the ways bad stress will alert you that it's been visiting for too long?

☐ Anxiety, anger, fear, or nervousness always seem just one step away.

☐ Headaches become commonplace.

☐ Normal sleep is a thing of the past; you are either staying awake until the wee hours because your mind won't shut off or sleeping far more than is normal for you.

☐ Concentration is nearly impossible.

☐ You have body aches that never seem to quit. They might even wander from place to place in your body.

☐ You snap at small things, reacting out of all proportion to a minor setback or challenge.

☐ Your appetite shifts. For some people it's being unable to eat; for others, it's compulsive overeating.

☐ Your drive sputters out before a task is completed.

☐ Your thought processes slow down; your mind grinds to a halt.

So what do you do when bad stress seems to have taken up permanent lodging with you? You stop. Right in your tracks. And you breathe. The faster you can pull yourself into the present moment, the more likely it is that stress can lose its hold on you for at least that little morsel of time. Focus on your hands, your shoes, or the view outside the window. Focus on *a thing*. Put your mind to work in objective observance. There is no stress in examining a tree branch, a shoelace, or a pencil.

When you break the cycle of stress-scream-scared-stress, it is easier to keep hyperstress at bay. If you look at the span of time from birth to where you are now, you'll realize that there have been other moments of stress, and you've gotten through those before. You can handle this one too—either by plowing through it, letting go of some of it, or walking away from it.

Instant Stressbusters

Get up and move. If you're already moving, move differently. Jump up and down. Do something that keeps you from thinking about your stress. Walk outside. Just the act of getting up from your seat and re-engaging with all your bones, muscles, and joints can move you into a different headspace.

Breathe. Dr. Andrew Weil has something called the "4-7-8 Breath" that is a relaxing breath. Trust me, I know from experience that when we are under enormous amounts of stress, we often forget to breathe. Breath is life. Please remember to breathe.

Grab your fur person. Hug them, wrestle with them, play fetch, play catch-the-catnip-mousie. Cats and dogs (as well as ferrets, guinea pigs, rabbits, and other small buddy critters) are some of the greatest stress-busters on the planet.

Meditate. Find some simple meditations you can tune into whenever the stress pulls you too tight. My absolute favorites are the ones by The Honest Guys, which you can find on YouTube for free. The meditations run anywhere from five minutes to several hours in length. If all you have time for is ten minutes, take the ten. You will undoubtedly ratchet down your pulse rate. If you're more of a reader type, I recommend *Soul Soothers: Mini Meditations for Busy Lives* by Cindy Griffith-Bennett. These meditations are just long enough for you to derail the mental crazymakers and bring yourself back in balance.

Sip something warm and comforting. Ditch the heavy stuff. Go for something soothing such as tea, cocoa, or soup. Take your time. Sip, don't gulp. Get into the aroma, the taste, and the savor.

Hug yourself. Really. Bow your head, close your eyes, put your arms around yourself, and breathe. Sometimes all we need is a loving touch to remind us we can make it through.

Find music that works for you. Listen to ambient or soothing music that calms you down. Perhaps it's bhangra because it peps you up. Maybe it's Broadway because those soaring voices become your voice. Whatever it is, if your music is your muse, feel free to indulge.

Set your boundaries. This stress buster is the most important thing you can do for yourself. You cannot work 24/7. You can't. You're not built that way. The more you grind your wheels, the more likely the wheels will come off at the least opportune time.

And as soon as it hits you that you simply aren't doing your best work, or that you can't concentrate, stop for now. Come back to the project or the list of to-dos when you can focus and get some of it done. Stretch. Remind yourself that life is supposed to be full of joy and want-tos, not have-tos.

The Adventure Pages:

Is Stress Good Or Bad?

Do you always think of stress as bad or are there times that stress has been good for you? When was a time you saw stress as good, and how did that work?

What are your particular "bad stress" triggers? How often do they happen?

What is your usual stress-busting behavior? Do you use it to stay on an even keel, or only when you think you're going to collapse?

What do you think could happen if you made time to clear stress, rather than let it build up? Where in your life would it make the biggest difference?

Put more arrows in your quiver: What three things do you want to take from this chapter and put to use in your life right now?

Here's your Invention Page!

Write down those three arrows on the blank page below. Draw, collage, or otherwise illustrate what your personal "Is Stress Good Or Bad? card" would look like.

Stress As the Shot Across the Bow

Okay, I'll admit it. I enjoy desserts, but not junk. It has to be *really* good; it's how I keep my consumption level down. That's why my favorite café and bakery, The Black Cat, is such a den of delicious deviousness in my book.

I was doing readings at The Black Cat one Saturday. It was well past noon, and the place was packed. I was reading client after client and hadn't eaten since very early that morning. I didn't want to bug the kitchen staff; they were behind as it was and people were pouring through the door. So I thought, "Heck, I'll just grab one of their raspberry bars." Now this is not *just* a raspberry bar; it's a piece of gustatorial Heaven, with a rich crust, perfect real raspberry filling, and a crumb topping. I pulled one off the baking tray in the kitchen. I wolfed it down and went back to reading.

In retrospect, it was probably two servings worth and hadn't been portioned out. But I was too busy, too stressed to notice.

Within the hour, my heart started to race as if it was training for the Kentucky Derby. I was shocked and thought to myself, *Why is this happening? What's going on?*

I took a wild guess that I might have had too much sugar in one sitting, and I went pelting over to my smartphone to get on the web. Sure enough, a hefty hit of concentrated sugar like that *can* and *does* up your heart rate, as well as your blood pressure.

Wow. Two things I already knew I needed to watch and, *boom*, I did a Double Dose of Stupid. All because I was too stressed to pay attention.

Now, I'd been told that "you shouldn't do sugar," and we all know that sugar is not the best thing to put in your body. But, I never took it too seriously until I got knocked in the head (or the pulse rate) with the incontrovertible proof.

So, from that point on, sugar became something really, *really* rare for me. I use sugar in my one cup of coffee in the morning because it's better than chemical alternatives. The rest of the day, I concentrate on taking in good quality protein, fruits and veggies, a little dairy, and nut butters. Desserts are relegated to Date Night, where Carle and I share one dessert, and I take just a few bites. On special occasions such as Valentine's Day and our anniversary—always celebrated at our favorite upscale restaurant—I may even indulge in an entire dessert just for me.

But, any other time, all I have to do is think about the terrifying feeling of my heart trying to jump out of my chest to remind myself that living healthy is better than a few mouthfuls of Demon Sweet.

That's your perfect example of "stress as a shot across the bow."

We talked about good stress versus bad stress in the previous chapter. Now we're going to talk about "stress as the shot across the bow." That particular phrase comes from naval parlance; it speaks of aiming a cannon shot across the bow of a ship, causing a small explosion in front of it and forcing it to stop. Nowadays, the phrase means "a warning to stop doing something."

It's one thing to pull the occasional all-nighter to finish your doctoral dissertation, plan a wedding, or open a business. Those are rare to one-time occurrences.

But when such time-crunch stresses are always front and center in your life, a shot across the bow is waiting to happen.

Jackie has three kids at home, ages two, six and eight. She also runs a small farm with her husband, which is how they make their living. She's up at dawn doing the family account books, working on herb drying, and getting the family in gear for the day. She sets Sally up in her play area and then starts homeschooling six-year-old Mike and eight-year-old Paige. In between these activities, Jackie continues farm chores and responds to customer requests on their online store.

"I love my kids, I really do," says Jackie. "But because I homeschool, there are constant demands on my time. I don't get the break from my kids that most parents do; they are in my face and space 24/7. And Mike and Sally are young enough that they don't understand boundaries the way they will when they're older. So I just—deal."

When she hasn't put any time aside for herself, Jackie runs out of patience and ideas. But she simply bites her lip, drinks another cup of coffee, and continues on.

Or she did until last November.

"Last fall, I just lost it," she admits. "I was on my fourth cup of coffee since 5 AM. Mike was arguing with me about why he had to weed the vegetable patch and water the goats *and* do his reading exercises. 'Farms are just dumb,' he yelled. 'I want to go to school like everyone else. Who cares about a farm, it's just dirt and smelly animals and I want to be rich and nobody gets rich on a farm!'

"Now, our farm is small, but it makes us a living. I gave up city living and *a lot* of luxuries to marry my husband and take on this project. It's important to me. But I was completely exhausted, at the end of my tether; I just didn't have it in me to explain it to Mike.

"I slapped him. I did what I swore I'd never do to one of my children. I started screaming at him, and I was shaking so badly that I knocked my coffee cup onto the flagstones. It crashed. Sally started shrieking and crying, frightened. Paige comes running in from the backyard, wanting to know what was wrong. She walks in to see me hysterical and her two siblings howling. And then Brendan, my husband, walks in, takes one look and asks me, 'What the hell happened?'

"I was so upset I couldn't even tell him at first. Paige took care of the littles while Brendan and I went out to the barn to talk. I finally admitted that I couldn't do all of it, something had to give."

That morning was Jackie's shot across the bow. She knew she wanted to be a good and loving mother. She wanted to see her kids homeschooled. She wanted to run her farm. How could it all get done? Jackie had to admit that she couldn't do it alone. She had to explore other alternatives and lift some of the burdens.

"There are other parents around here who homeschool," she said, "but I never thought of them as a resource. I thought everyone was as stressed as I was." Jackie and Brendan reached out to the half-dozen families in the area who were also home-schoolers, and there is now an ad hoc group that co-teaches. It means that Paige and Mike actually go to their neighbors' homes for lessons three days a week. One day a week, Jackie has another six children to teach what she knows and loves: science (her college double major was ecology and biology). Mike is happier with more socialization time. And he is learning just how "cool" living on a farm looks to the other kids.

"It's made a huge difference for all of us," Jackie sighs gratefully. "I have a little time to myself now. I don't feel as pressured. The kids are happier, which means I'm happier. But if I hadn't lost it that morning last fall, I have no idea if we would have ever made the necessary changes. I was just too immersed in the next crisis to see what was needed."

For both Jackie and me, the unrelenting stress, which had gone unchecked, resulted in situations that woke us up to the damage that loomed in the future. In my case, it was serious health compromises. In Jackie's situation, it was emotional and family fracturing. But both of us also saw that "shot across the bow" as a wake-up call to look at our lives and make the changes we needed to get through the long haul happily and productively, without sacrificing either ourselves or our families.

Look at your own life right now. How many places does stress take precedence over what you think you should (or know you *need* to) do for yourself? How often does that happen?

If it's more than once in a blue moon, that's your shot across the bow. Time to trim your sails and change your course.

You can do so by looking at the circumstances that brought about the shot:

☐ What can you change?

☐ What can you let go?

☐ Who do you have around you—whether family, neighbors or others –that can help you realign what's going on?

☐ Most importantly, where have you been so stubborn, so fixated, that you allowed this to happen?

Answering those four questions can turn the Ship of You around, sailing away from the stressmakers. And if a ship doesn't sail in a certain direction, the shot across the bow isn't in close range. (That's the whole idea around "smooth sailing," no?)

The shot across the bow is *always* the first shot, and it's always just a warning. Be sure to take heed so that the next shot doesn't take down your Life-Boat entirely.

The Adventure Pages:

Stress As the Shot Across the Bow

When was the last time that a stress event gave you a massive wake-up call? What happened?

What do you keep saying you can't change that you know you can—and must—for your own or for another's sake? What would it take for you to make those changes?

What can you do for yourself to help ratchet down the biggest stressor you currently have?

Put more arrows in your quiver: What three things do you want to take from this chapter and put to use in your life right now?

Here's your Invention Page!

Write down those three arrows on the blank page below. Draw, collage, or otherwise illustrate what your personal "Stress as A Shot Across the Bow card" would look like.

Stress As Mission Creep

When stress appears as the shot across the bow, it's one of those instant-wake-up moments that help us change our lives. But stress isn't always that direct or dramatic. Sometimes it sneaks up on us until we turn around and find it staring us in the face. When that happens, it requires us to take it by the scruff of the neck and march it back out the door.

Ramona's situation is a perfect example of "stress as mission creep." From childhood, Ramona had been a passionate and talented knitter. Even now, at the end of a long office workday, she liked nothing better than to tuck into her favorite chair and relax with her yarn bag. In her hands the needles flew, and beautiful creations seemed to tumble from them like magic. So, when a friend asked if she would make a few baby items for the local homeless shelter, Ramona was happy to oblige.

Then, someone at the shelter saw her work and asked if she might make a few more for their fundraiser. After all, this was for homeless mothers and children.

"Could you make them in a few different colors?"

Ramona said yes. She purchased extra yarn and set aside more time in the evenings.

The local public television station did a piece on the shelter fundraiser, and the reporter loved the knitted baby things. The station contacted her about their fund drive—after all, she was a member. And so they asked Ramona, "Please can you make just a few more...and could they be in this particular pattern with organic yarn from one of our underwriters?"

Ramona suddenly found herself inundated with deadlines, specific colors and patterns, different yarn requirements, and commitments that went far beyond the comfortable and relaxing time that an evening's knitting was *supposed* to be. But she had said yes, yes, and yes, when it had all seemed so very reasonable—and she felt she couldn't back out of her commitments.

When it was all done, a year and a half later, she put away her knitting and never went back. Knitting had gone from something relaxing to dealing with just another piece of stress. That's a classic example of "stress as mission creep."

Mission creep is a military term. I asked a friend of mine, a long-time Air Force man, to define this term for the book. He laughed. "Mission creep is when projects or goals, which are beyond the original objectives, are added to an operation. Sometimes it happens organically in a unit, and sometimes it's inflicted by higher echelons, where senior officers get so-called good ideas. Sometimes mission creep can be harmless. Sometimes it can completely derail the primary mission."

That's exactly what happened with Ramona. Her knitting was impeccable and so Ramona appreciated that more and more people asked for her help and for her work. Like the frog in a pot of slowly heating water, she didn't realize she was overextended until it was too late to escape the circumstances without breaking her word to a number of people. And it transformed something that had been a favorite pastime to becoming just one more stressful task to check off her list.

Ramona's knitting conundrum is another version of not understanding our boundaries and not taking care of ourselves. There are some stresses we can't avoid: a boss who micromanages, a house full of children, financial ups-and-downs, world political tensions that affect us—whether indirectly or directly. We don't actively invite those stressors into our lives, but they happen, and they're a part of today's world.

When we don't think carefully about our time and we fail to take care of ourselves, then the small requests for our time and resources can become demands before we know it. Many people can see someone's good nature or talents and reason with themselves, "I can ask him to do one thing, it's not a problem."

Here's another way to look at it.

Museums are amazing places. They are doorways into the past, showing us who we were and how we got to be where we are now. And in many museums, artifacts are put on display close enough to touch.

☐ A wedding gown for a very small woman from 1835, the lace fraying and fragile.

☐ A fire engine from the 18th century, all wood and metal and holding the memories of centuries.

☐ A corn-husk doll with a fading calico dress that

saw Indian raids and rough living with its little mothering child.

Everywhere, these precious items beckon you, whispering "Learn about us. Find out about us." But, there are signs in museums that read "Please do not touch," and there are good reasons for every one of them.

My husband runs a Revolutionary War museum with eight different buildings. Each one has a version of those signs. And this is because the items on exhibit are no longer the fresh, robust makings that they were in years gone by. Time has taken its toll. Therefore, that simple request is made so that all may wonder at them, enjoy them, and learn from them.

Yet, invariably, someone says to themselves, *Oh, one touch won't matter.* And they reach out over the barricade to finger these precious pieces of the past. They tug on a bowstring to see how strong it was. They flip the sleeve of a gown to see how it was made. They run their hands along the peeling paint of a harpsichord, and tentatively finger one or another of the yellowed keys.

Now, imagine that happening month after month, year after year, by far more than *one* person. Because one person felt they could ignore the rules, and then another and another, these treasures are marred, damaged, and corrupted by dirt and the body oils of those who touched them. Eventually, these artifacts are taken off display to preserve them against those that thought the rules did not apply to them. As a result, the wonder of them is denied to everyone— even those who respected the rules and requests.

That's another version of "stress as mission creep." One touch may not matter, but the whole will build up until the object collapses under the stress of contact, contaminants, and a lack of understanding about how to preserve artifacts.

How to Avoid "Stress As Mission Creep" In Your Own Life

Be aware of time commitments. I know in my life, as my career has taken off and more and more days are filled with clients and writing, I can't be there as much for long phone conversations or spontaneous days off or holding to promises wheedled out of me. True friends understand that it's not a lack of caring that we don't chat on the phone for an hour anymore, and it doesn't mean I don't support their charities or activities. It is simply that I have a 24-hour day—as does everyone else—and more of it is committed than used to be. It also means I make darn sure that any extra time I have fulfills me in some way: either through direct self-care or doing something with and for people or groups that truly matter to me.

Think carefully before you say yes. In fact, delay. In my younger days, it was a given that I'd join a group and within a month I'd be one of the officers or otherwise acquire massive responsibilities. Why? I'll be blunt. I am a natural leader type with a strong personality, and the ability to take command of a situation and get it done. It's why I never enjoyed anything for very long. I never gave myself a chance to have fun and learn about a group before running it. As a result, I would leave after a year or two, feeling unfulfilled and tired. What looked like it would be tremendous fun turned out to be just one more responsibility I didn't need.

When someone asks you for a favor or a time commitment or anything that might cause stress, *never* automatically agree. Say, "Let me check my schedule and get back to you" or "I don't want to say yes until I know I can follow through, I'll let you know." If they repeatedly push to get you to say "Yes" before you are ready, then you know they are not thinking of you or the project, but of themselves. They will not respect your time or your no. In that case, your answer should be a flat, "No, sorry." Then, stick to your guns about it.

Understand that guilt is useless for everybody. Clients often tell me, "I really didn't want to do it, but I felt guilty after I said I would." Another version is, "I felt so guilty about saying no; I didn't want to look selfish."

Guilt is an utterly worthless emotion. It doesn't feel good to you. It is usually used as a weapon or a goad by someone who wants to control and manipulate. It doesn't give you any extra energy; in fact, it saps energy from you. When you catch someone trying to guilt you into a commitment, remember another wonderful military phrase: "Tactic perceived is no tactic."

If you see clearly that someone is using guilt as a motivator, call them on it. "Jeanne, I know you want me to go with you to the nursing home tomorrow. I know you hate having to see your mother on your own. But you're trying to guilt me into going, and it isn't going to work. That will push me away from future trips, rather than get me to come with you another time. Accept my no this time gracefully, and perhaps I'll be able to say yes in the future." Say this kindly, reasonably, but firmly. And watch the reaction.

If the person trying to guilt you into doing something denies their actions or gets mad, that's a huge indicator that they are not likely to be someone who reduces your stress. So you may want to rethink any commitments with them at all.

Conversely, don't use guilt on yourself as a motivator. If you need to do something, and you no longer want to, you can certainly acknowledge that. But buckle down and do what you can. Remember that the sooner you get it done, the sooner you will be able to say no to it next time.

If Ramona had understood "stress as mission creep," she would have stuck with making baby clothes for the shelter and said no to the other requests. I would have sat on my hands instead of raising them to volunteer all the time during my younger years. And perhaps those museum visitors would have kept their hands to themselves, and enjoyed the artifacts by merely observing and asking questions of the docents by the exhibits.

These days, the world puts enough stress on our plate; it's not usually something we enjoy. Make sure you don't ask for second helpings by saying yes to more things than you can handle comfortably, no matter how much people beleaguer you to do so.

The Adventure Pages:

Stress As Mission Creep

What was the last thing you enjoyed that became a burden because you didn't say "no" or mark out boundaries?

Who in your life constantly ups your stress? Do they do it out of manipulation, victimhood, self-interest or something else? Ask yourself: *Are they worth keeping?* If so, how can you change the balance?

Of our three "mission creep avoidance strategies," which one do you most need to apply in your life? Why?

Put more arrows in your quiver: What three things do you want to take from this chapter and put to use in your life right now?

Here's your Invention Page!

Write down those three arrows on the blank page below. Draw, collage, or otherwise illustrate what your personal "Stress as Mission Creep card" would look like.

Stress, the Donkey, and the Hole In the Ground

There's a folk tale that most people know very well, which involves an old, blind donkey. He'd served his farmer for many years. But now, in his owner's opinion, he was doing nothing more than eating and taking up space. The farmer had little patience for those who could not do a good day's work.

One day, the farmer heard piteous cries and went out to his field, where he noticed the blind donkey had fallen into a deep hole in the ground. "Well," thought the farmer, "he's not worth bringing back up. Maybe this is my chance to get rid of him." And so the farmer called the farm hands to him. They each brought a shovel and callously began to fling dirt in the hole, assuming they could bury the donkey alive. The donkey's shrieks grew louder and louder. Then—silence. The farmer assumed that his plan was working, so he continued to shovel in the dirt.

Imagine their surprise when the donkey climbed out of the hole on the pile of dirt they had thrown in, intending to kill him. Instead, it saved his life. And it proved to the farmer that a donkey with that much grit and brains really did deserve to live.

For me, this models the idea of "one step at a time" and Living the Examined Life. Stress can be absolutely overwhelming. We can have so much on our plate. And so much more seems to be piling itself on top of us, with no way of getting out from under, that we panic. We find ourselves paralyzed. When we look at what is in front of us in the present moment and put aside other things until we can get one thing solved, we find we can breathe more easily.

When I originated this chapter, I was living the donkey story. Major surgery was looming, which meant I would be completely unable to work for at least two weeks. My website revision was due to go up in two days, and there was still much work to be done. Financially, I had medical bills ahead, doctors' fees to cover, and vet fees for the cats. All of these pressures were happening at once when I would be unable to work. And, to top it off, I was having spells of vertigo with no idea why.

I could have sat at my desk and panicked. Instead, I looked at the calendar, examined each situation, and then assessed what I *could* do. When I looked at one thing at a time, other things did attempt to crowd in, yes; but I was able to push them back into place and decide what I could handle and what I couldn't.

How To Triage Your Stress

Mary Kay Ash, the doyenne of pinkitude who created Mary Kay Cosmetics, was very fond of saying, "You can even eat an elephant a teaspoonful at a time." She was right. Sometimes things cannot go the way you want them to. But rather than stress about it, look at the reality of the situation and work with what you have—one piece at a time.

For example, Robin was one of my best friends in high school. When I would be front stage during our dramatic productions, she would be backstage: acting as stage manager, executive assistant to the director, and everybody's problem solver. In her 20s and 30s, she was wardrobe captain for several famous rock bands and her city's opera company, and ultimately landed the plum position of handling the gowns and glitter for a big Motown star who was a world traveler. But eventually, she tired of the road warrior work and settled into being a terrific mom. She never lost her ability to juggle more tasks than most of us could imagine, let alone competently handle.

There was one time Robin thought Life with all its stresses was definitely going to defeat her. She was feeling overwhelmed, pulled in many directions. Her daughter Connie was trying to choose among three local colleges and needed to finalize her decision within ten days. Connie wanted to go back and visit all three before she made her choice. Robin's work with the Big Brothers Big Sisters organization, where she was event coordinator, meant she was under the gun; its huge annual fundraiser was in eight days' time and the caterer they had planned to use called with the news that his entire restaurant had burned down the night before and would be unable to fulfill his contract. The family's Akita/Shepherd cross, Muttso, was losing weight and could not eat; a trip to the vet (and all the recurrent expenses) was imminent. And, in the middle of everything, Robin's doctor called to say that her blood tests were in, and he wanted her to make an appointment that week regarding some abnormal findings.

Is it any wonder Robin was ready to jump off the local bridge? Robin absolutely knew that there was no way all of this could be handled alone. But she had to make her list of priorities. "For me, it was A-B-C," she laughs, remembering that crazed week. "A meant I *had* to do it; B meant I really *would have liked* to do it; and C meant 'in your dreams, bucko.'" She knew she had to take things one at a time or she would never be able to face them all. And if there were a chance to pass off some of the items, she would.

"The first thing I did, frankly, was to call my ex. He's Connie's dad, he's very involved in her life, and they get along really well. He said that he could take her to the colleges for a final review. So that was off my plate. Then, Muttso went to the vet. When it's an animal, you don't know if it's serious or not; they can't tell you. I asked to leave him for two days for their tests and to get him out from under my feet while I handled the rest of the crises. Believe it or not, the next thing I did was call the doctor and ask, 'Am I dying here, or can it wait until next week?' Turns out that *abnormal* wasn't anything serious, just a blip up in my cholesterol, and I wasn't going to be admitted to a hospital because of it. So I made an appointment for three weeks out, and he didn't object.

"That left me free to handle the biggest crisis: the fundraiser. It's almost impossible to get a caterer for feeding 1,300 people in a week! It took several phone calls by both the caterer who had the fire and me, but we managed. Two interviews, two food sample tastings, and we squeaked in under the wire. We even got our deposit back from the fellow who was supposed to be doing the gig, which we didn't expect.

"If I had tried to do all of that at once, nothing would have gotten done. I would have collapsed, everything would have gone to hell in a hand-basket, and I would have blamed myself for it for weeks, whether it made sense or not.

"I learned a long time ago that I don't have to solve everything. If I look at things squarely, one at a time, I can see what I need to do and what can be put aside until I have a moment to breathe."

Back to the donkey and the farmer.

The donkey didn't see if he could figure out where the next shovel of dirt was coming from. He didn't waste time feeling betrayed by all the farm hands he'd helped out over the years. Eventually, he didn't even waste his breath braying. He saw his opportunity and took it, a shovel of dirt at a time. Focused only on what he could control in the moment and not wasting a minute on what had or would happen in a few minutes, the donkey took his chance with what was going on right then. And it got him out of the hole and into a much more comfortable existence.

Like the donkey, you can "step up" to task after task, but you need to focus on one thing at a time. If you're faced with times when you simply can't do everything and can't find help, go back to the A-B-C list that Robin uses. Do what you absolutely must. If you have time, do the "B" list items. And the rest? Forgive yourself for leaving them by the wayside. Life doesn't always make room for everything we want—or what people want from us.

There are times when Fate hands a bunch of its buddies a passel of shovels. Dirt—in the form of tasks, problems, crises, major decisions—comes flinging at us from all directions. When it does, we have two choices: we can either bray piteously at The Unfairness of It All and let it bury us, or we can stop braying and start stepping. One pile of dirt, one solved crisis at a time. And when you step out of that "hole" that others couldn't imagine defeating, people will wonder how they ever doubted you in the first place.

The Adventure Pages:

Stress, the Donkey, and the Hole In the Ground

What was the last situation that overwhelmed you? Why?

Had you implemented the A-B-C priority list, what do you believe would have happened instead?

If someone said to you, "You don't need to solve everything" regarding an important situation, how would you feel? Would you change your actions as a result? How so?

Put more arrows in your quiver: What three things do you want to take from this chapter and put to use in your life right now?

Here's your Invention Page!

Write down those three arrows on the blank page below. Draw, collage, or otherwise illustrate what your personal "Stress, the Donkey, and the Hole In the Ground card" would look like.

Conclusion

When you came looking for a book like this one, you were probably dissatisfied with your LifeCloset: full of ideas and beliefs from your past that were put there by well-meaning parents, competitive siblings, earnest friends, frenemies, work situations, romantic partners both good and bad, and all you've experienced living in this big, complicated world. And you picked up this volume because whatever was in that closet was no longer what you wanted. You thought there might be some new ideas in here that work.

Now here you are, at the tail end of the pages you started exploring with hope and curiosity not long ago. If this book has resonated with you, here are some of the ways you might have already experienced change:

☐ You've gotten clear on what you want to bring into your life.

☐ You've looked at what you have and decided what is useful and worth keeping.

☐ You've tossed aside that which doesn't serve you.

☐ You've even learned that you can adapt some of what's around you to bring you what you want.

☐ You've learned how to deal with inevitable stress so that you handle it rather than it handling you.

☐ Most importantly, you've learned to trust your own knowing about things.

How do I know? Because you've stuck with me through this whole self-quest, and you're still reading.

Throughout these pages, I've reminded you time and again that YOU are your own best expert. Let's be honest: I can give you examples of what I've seen and done. I can share lists with you that I have found useful. I can even tell you reassuring stories about how I got through some very tough times that may look a lot like what you've gone through yourself.

But unless these stories and examples resonate with you, they are not equipment to put in your LifeCloset.

What goes back into your LifeCloset are those beliefs, ideas, methods and tips that will support the life you want to bring into being. That's why The Adventure Pages at the end of each chapter are so important (and if you didn't do those activities, trust me: you want to go back and dig in). They were designed to be the place where you go to play around with my ideas and make them delightfully, uniquely yours.

And when you've closed this book and settled it back on your shelf, what happens then? That's when the fun really begins. Go, my friend. Go and try out all those ideas on your world.

Look at your life with more clarity. Know where that telescope—cleaned and polished and aimed to a fare-thee-well—can catch a glimpse of all the promise that is yours in the future, no matter your age or your circumstances.

You will have cleared out all of those raggedy thoughts, outworn principles, too-small life plans and directions that were never yours in the first place but bequeathed to you by others. You'll recognize them for what they are: poorly-fitting hand-me-downs that don't need to take up precious space.

You'll have lightened your load—disposing of anything you no longer need, which no longer supports you. That leaves room and time to cherish what is precious. You'll start looking for experiences, not "stuff." And you'll have passed on some of those ideas, things, and experiences to those who will treasure them.

You'll have practiced living your life like the best of chefs, making sumptuous days and weeks out of what is presented to you by Spirit. You'll understand the deliciousness of making perfection out of imperfection. You'll understand that stumbling is actually part of the Big Dance. And you will have a solid understanding of when adaptability is not useful, but a big fat "No" is.

You'll get a grip on stress. You'll be able to differentiate between good and bad stress. You'll recognize when it's real and when it's not. You'll work out how to turn matters away if they aren't your problem to solve. And though stress is and always will be a part of your life, you won't let it bury you.

You'll be ready for *The Big Reboot*, which will be Volume II of *The Self-Development Project*.

The biggest change that I would wish for you, now that we've walked together, is a simple one: Own the fact that you are in charge of your own existence. Not the Fates. Not your financial circumstances. Not your family or your birth or your gender. You. Knowing that you are the captain of your own ship means you can decide how to steer it through the waters of your existence. Sometimes those waters will make for smooth sailing, and sometimes they will be so rough you will be pea-green in the face and hanging over the edge of the deck. But you will still be the captain. You get to claim your own triumphs and recognize your own miscalculations. Either way, you are in charge, and that means all possibilities are yours as well.

Lastly, I want to thank you. Yes, really. Not just for buying or reading the book, but for being someone who wanted to take the same journey as I did. You can't write what you don't know, so I had to live every single chapter of this book before getting it down on paper.

Clarity for me meant knowing who I was and what I was here to do. It meant getting rid of all those things that I allowed to stop me before. I had to jettison self-doubt, an insurmountable mountain of half-formed ideas I'd no idea how to finish, and the constant urge to put myself last because everyone else needed more. I had to be willing to dump the excuses: waiting until the timing was perfect, or until I was well-known enough, or until a big publishing house would magnanimously give me permission to be *in a book*. And it meant I had to let go of all that self-imposed stress—or this manuscript would never have gotten finished.

You can do what I do because I had to do what I've asked you to do. And there are so many more delicious adventures to experience together!

Wingfolks

Think about those breathtaking V formations of Canadian Geese that you see every spring and fall. The flocks fly hundreds of miles to get to their seasonal nesting grounds—but they can't do it without supporting each other. That's what these suggested peripherals are all about: getting wonderful support as you get to work cleaning out that Life-Closet. (And if you see something mentioned here, I have read or used it and can recommend it from personal experience.)

Law of Attraction: The Science of Getting More of What You Want and Less of What You Don't by Michael Losier. This is the Law of Attraction book I recommend over all others.

Askfirmations: Live the Life You Desire Simply by Asking by Christine Alexandria. I adore Christine. She has taken every idea about affirmations and turned it inside out. Askfirmations beat affirmations hands down in terms of instantly changing energy.

Soul Soothers: Mini Meditations for Busy Lives by Cindy Griffith-Bennett. Cindy is a personal friend with a great heart that understands practicality as well as high metaphysics. These are little one-page meditations that can be practiced throughout the day wherever you are. Cindy speaks to Everyman and Everywoman, so no matter where you are in your spiritual journey, you'll find something useful in this delightful little tome.

Stumbling Toward Enlightenment and **Building a Business the Buddhist Way** by Geri Larkin. Geri Larkin is mentioned prominently in this volume. Go enjoy her work for yourself.

To Love Is to Be Happy With and **Happiness is a Choice** by Barry Neil Kaufman. These are the books that got me through three bouts of breast cancer, two divorces, and the deaths of my parents. Kaufman's Option Process® Dialogue and the Option Institute where it is taught have changed my life immeasurably since 1983.

Your Soul's Plan: Discovering the Real Meaning of the Life You Planned Before You Were Born and **Your Soul's Gift: The Healing Power of the Life You Planned Before You Were Born** by Robert Schwartz. If you want to understand pre-birth planning and Karma from a very compassionate standpoint, these are your books. I was one of the channels and mediums that Schwartz used in these volumes, and my own cancer story is in the first one under the pseudonym of "Doris." I am incredibly proud of being part of this series.

Garden of One Vibrational Essences. The products by long-time Vibrational Alchemist Rachel Ginther shift and transform the energy patterns that keep you bound to old behaviors and beliefs that no longer serve you. The kit we suggest is her Gentle Goodbye Essence Kit: gracefully disengage from patterns, relationships, and situations that limit your personal and spiritual growth and awareness. Get the kit at bit.ly/gentlegoodbyeessencekit or visit gardenofnone.com.

Hemi-Sync®. Hemi-Sync® can help you experience enhanced mental, physical, and emotional states by combining verbal guidance, music, pink sound and/or other audio effects with the binaural beats. The particular elements for each recording are carefully selected and integrated with the appropriate Hemi-Sync® sound frequencies to enhance the desired effect. Visit hemi-sync.com.

Brain Sync®. Brain Sync® audio programs combine guided meditation, subliminal messaging and advanced brainwave entrainment techniques to leverage your brain power so that you can achieve the goals you set for yourself. EEG studies conducted at Duke University concluded that binaural beats have the potential to affect mood and performance. For thirty years, Kelly Howell, founder of Brain Sync, has worked with eminent brain researchers, and scientists to create the best binaural beat audios available in the world today. Learn more at brainsync.com.

Aknowledgements

Adam Crafter and Laura Knight. Thank you for being the first to taste the idea of the book and pronounce it delicious.

Bears and Samahria Kaufman, and all the Master Teachers I have known through the years at the Option Institute. Thank you for being an anchor-point and beacon of possibility for me for over three decades.

Bernadette Carter-King. You are a force of nature who swept in and showed me the Golden Rules of Friendship in every way. Thank you for believing in me.

Berni Xiong. You are a superb editor and a Fierce Bookbear. Your clear-eyed assessment finally lit the rocket pack on my back to get this book into print.

Chris Alexandria. Thank you—and all of your angels—for helping me to reimagine The Self-Development Project in a more playful way.

McKittycreek's Baron Manfred and Shubacoons' Captain Oswald. Every Momcat-writer needs a kid (or two) to remind her to breathe... purr...play. And no cat teaches that better than a Maine Coon.

Robert Schwartz. You offered me the chance to do greater works than I could have imagined, when neither one of us had any idea what was ahead of us. Thank you. You are indeed a Courageous Soul yourself.

Shirley Dorkin, my stepmother, who loved me like I was her own and believed in me and my singular Path—even when no one else in the family knew how.

Staci Wells. Thank you for being a fabulous intuitive, a trusted colleague, and a friend who never fails to amaze me.

Steve Bhaerman, otherwise known as Swami Beyondananda. Thank you for being my favorite no-hoodoo-guru, demonstrating so deliciously how to take humor seriously, and seriousness humorously.

Wendy and Richard Pini. For thirty years you have been senseis, friends and pack leaders who understood when it was time for me to howl on my own trails. A bow of respect to you, and an ocean of thanks.

My husband, Carle Kopecky. Even after many years, I am awed and grateful to have you as my lifemate. With you, I laugh. I look more deeply into what I want to create in the world. You are steadfast, loving, protective, honest, true. You are everything I ever wanted for myself, even before I knew that's what I wanted. Thank you for being. I love you.

About the Author

Corbie Mitleid has always been "the different one." A writer and visionary in a completely medical family (father a doctor, mother a nurse, brother a doctor), she has always made her own path rather than take one cut for her by others. Leaving an Ivy League university after two years, Corbie struck out to find where joy and purpose lived, regardless of what she was told she "ought" to do.

The path wasn't easy. Two marriages, which didn't last, and a constant search for The Partner Who Understood. A succession of jobs. A series of spiritual paths. Moving from Cambridge to Philadelphia to Poughkeepsie to New York City to Atlanta. Out of the blue, breast cancer—not once, but three times. Life became a roller coaster with no brakes, asking Corbie to survive divorce, abuse, poverty and life-threatening illness. But through all of this, she learned the value of the Examined Life: meeting challenges and always asking the next question, facing each new situation with strength, courage and humor.

Today, Corbie brings a full toolbox to her job as a beacon of manifestation and vision for her clients. She knows what it is to create a career out of experiences. While she's now a full-time intuitive counselor and inspirational speaker, her career has encompassed positions as a published author, a professional actress, a television producer, a radio personality, an executive recruiter and the "power behind the throne" for a number of high-profile CEOs.

Corbie's career now spans the globe, with clients worldwide. Her talents as an intuitive are featured in bestselling books. Still, her clients treasure her attitude of *I'm not special, you can do what I do.*

"We have opportunities we can go after, and challenges to get past," she says firmly. "My job is to give you the tools and courage to deal with both situations. Everything else is free will, and up to you!"

Corbie lives in upstate New York with her husband Carle, a museum director, and three large and exuberant Maine Coon cats.

※ ※ ※

If you want to find out more about this book, and sign up for **The Self Development Insider**, go to cleanoutyourlifecloset.com.

You can also "Like" and share **The Self-Development Project** page on Facebook at https://www.facebook.com/TSDPBookSeries.

To leave an honest review and star rating, go to the book's listing on Amazon.com.

Watch for *The Self-Development Project* Volumes II and III.